W9-BOA-266

61 - 69

A Reader's Guide to

English & American

Literature

A Reader's Guide to
English & American
Literature

LIBRARY
BRYAN COLLEGE
DAYTON, TENN. 37321

Andrew Wright

University of California

San Diego

Library
Bryan College
Dayton. Tennessee 37321

Scott, Foresman and Company

29566

Library of Congress Catalog Card No. 70-115334.

Copyright © 1970 by Scott, Foresman and Company, Glenview, Illinois 60025.
Philippines Copyright 1970 by Scott, Foresman and Company.
All Rights Reserved. Printed in the United States of America.

Regional offices of Scott, Foresman and Company are located in Atlanta, Dallas, Glenview, Palo Alto, Oakland, N.J., and London, England.

Preface

A Reader's Guide to English and American Literature is an intentionally exclusive list, a key for those readers who want to be shown the way to the most reliable editions of the principal authors and the best works of biography and criticism. It is also a guide to the most useful works of reference, in the fields of English and American literature especially, and to a number of foreign literatures as well. Over against the bewildering proliferation of books and books about books, the present compilation claims the virtue of selectivity. The ordinary reader of Shakespeare does not want to bury himself under all the thousands of works—major, minor, specialized, curious, eccentric—that have been written about him: the ordinary reader wants to be able to find out about such fine guides as *The Reader's Encyclopedia of Shakespeare,* a wonderfully useful compendium. By the same token, the ordinary reader of George Eliot does not want to be treated to a list of all the books written about the author of *Adam Bede* and *Middlemarch:* he wants to know about the three or four works that say the most intelligent and helpful things about the subject.

Of the arrangement of *A Reader's Guide* a word should be said. English literature comes first, and commences with a listing of general works under such headings as "Guides to Literary Study," "Reference Works," "Literary History," "Language," and so on. There follow listings under conventional headings of the principal works by and about the principal authors.

The arrangement within the period headings begins with general lists, of works of literary and other kinds of history, and of anthologies useful to the reader. Then follow lists of works by and about the principal authors. The arrangement here is chronological, by year of birth. Future literary historians and bibliographers may choose to smile at the division into literary periods (the Middle English Period is so long, the Romantic Period so short) and at the choice of authors (why Southey? why not John Barth?), but I have aimed at being merely conventional in the setting forth of categories here, and also in the choice of authors represented. This *Reader's Guide* is no place for revolutions. Equally conventional is the style in which the names of the writers are listed: I have used the forms evidently preferred by themselves. For the books included short titles are used, unless the full title says something so useful that it must be exhibited.

Where anything like a complete edition of an author's works exists I have listed it, even though it may be long out of print and therefore accessible only in a good library. Of course I have listed editions of scholarly eminence, such as the Herford and Simpson Ben Jonson, the California Dryden, and the Ohio State Hawthorne. I have also felt it my duty to point to some of the most outstanding works available in paperbound versions, but I have been selective rather than exhaustive.

In separating works of biography from works of criticism I have been conscious at every point of drawing lines where boundaries are dangerous if not forbidden. The relationship between an author's life and what he writes is bound to be intimate, even if (as is true of Shakespeare) little is known about his life, even if (as is true of Milton) he is austerely impersonal in his choice of subject matter, even if (as is true of Jane Austen) he is self-effacing. But it has seemed to me useful to distinguish where distinction is possible, for there are times when one wants to look up the facts, so far as they can be known, of an author's life, as one can do in William Riley Parker's *Milton,* Edgar Johnson's *Charles Dickens,* and a number of other standard biographies. But there are authors whose biographies remain to be written, sometimes because their biographical circumstances are closely intertwined with those of their works: such an author is Samuel Richardson, to whom life and art—see his letters—became practically indistinguishable. In such cases I have had to combine my categories, reluctantly but frankly.

A large class of secondary works has been excluded: essays published in journals and (for the most part) essays published in miscellanies of one sort or another. As for the former, I have nearly persuaded myself that all or almost all really first-class fugitive essays eventually appear in book form; but it is less easy to be convinced that Lionel Trilling's collections of essays should be excluded (though many of them do appear in other kinds of collections listed in these pages). All I can plead is the fear of multiplying titles, such that English and American literature would be buried rather than praised.

Some of the books listed here are better than others—some, indeed, which are not very good at all, have been listed for lack of better. But the bibliographer is at the mercy of literary fashion. Several first-class books have been written about James Joyce, but a really outstanding book of criticism about Smollett has yet to appear. Accordingly, the listings under such attractive authors as Joyce (and Milton, Fielding, Pope, Yeats, and T. S. Eliot) have had to be privative, omitting works of outstanding but specialized value so that the user of the compilation would not confuse forest and trees. Other writers have been less fortunate in their biographers and critics, and I have simply listed the best works known to me.

A concluding note of modesty is in order. I am all too aware that omnicompetence is not to be achieved even in the making of bibliographies. In putting together those which appear in the present volume I have used my own judgment, of course, but I have also learned gratefully from the work of others, especially those whose bibliographical handbooks are listed here, and also my colleagues at the San Diego campus of the University of California, who have let me know, vive voce, what they think of my lists.

Contents

The Earlier Seventeenth Century (to 1660)   30

The Restoration and the Eighteenth Century (1660–1800)   44

The Romantic Period (1800–1830)   66

The Victorian Age (1830–1890)   77

The Early Modern Period (1890–1920)   90

The Recent Past (1920–1960)   98

American Literature   109

General   110

Colonial and Revolutionary America to 1800   115

The Nineteenth Century   120

The Twentieth Century   136

General, Classical, and Modern European History and Literature   159

Introduction

Cookbooks very often begin with a *batterie de cuisine,* a more-or-less imposing list of utensils necessary to perform the arts of cookery. Bibliographies seldom begin so engagingly or so usefully. In fact, as reading is a solitary enterprise it requires privacy—a room of one's own if possible—and a certain minimum of utensils. Every reader needs at least a modest shelf of reference books at hand, so that he can look up the meaning of words, trace allusions, track down mythological references, explore areas opened up in the book before him. To assemble such a collection is easy and amusing: readers of books generally like books themselves, and the bookshops, especially second-hand bookshops, can be made to yield up treasures at prices that are far from outrageous. The purpose of the following paragraphs is to recommend a number of reference works that will help the reader of literature get full enjoyment and value from his books.

The first requisite, of course, is dictionaries; and at the top of the list is a desk-size dictionary, of which the new *American Heritage Dictionary* is the most up-to-date and probably the most worthwhile if a new book is to be bought. But a second-hand volume can do most of the jobs a dictionary is wanted for: I have a 1949 Merriam-Webster *New Collegiate Dictionary,* given to me by the G. & C. Merriam Company when I was an instructor at Ohio State University a number of years ago—and it remains splendidly useful. Of course the newest edition (1963) is more up-to-date and is to be preferred for that reason; but the by now middle-aged *New Collegiate* is not to be despised. My only objection to it is that the brief biographies appear in a separate alphabetical list rather than being incorporated in the main body of the dictionary itself. This, however, is a small price to pay for a work that is otherwise fine. It would be wrong, however, to give a blanket endorsement to all collegiate dictionaries; a number of the drug-store models (including those with "Webster," that magic word in lexicographical circles, on the title page) are worse than useless. The following, not generally obtainable in drug stores, are to be recommended in addition to the two already remarked on: *The American College Dictionary* (New York, 1962), *Funk & Wagnalls Standard College Dictionary* (New York, 1963), the Random House *Dictionary of the English Language, College Edition* (New York, 1968), the *Thorndike-Barnhart Comprehensive Desk Dictionary*

(Garden City, New York, 1962), and *Webster's New World Dictionary* (Cleveland, 1962).

But every reader needs dictionaries more comprehensive than any of the desk-size volumes. At the least it is desirable to have *The Shorter Oxford English Dictionary,* that excellent abridgment of what is undoubtedly the best dictionary in the language, *The Oxford English Dictionary,* a thirteen-volume compilation that is out of reach of many pockets. *The Shorter Oxford* is published in a one-volume and also in a two-volume edition—the only difference is the thickness of the paper used; the text is identical. The great value of *The Shorter Oxford* is that, like its parent, it not only defines words lucidly but also cites examples from literary, historical, and philosophical documents, of actual usage. *The Shorter Oxford* is in print and can be bought new for $32.00. (*The Oxford English Dictionary* is also in print and can be bought for $300.00. It makes a fine graduation or wedding present, and is virtually unobtainable second hand.) Another work I often have recourse to is Eric Partridge's *Dictionary of Slang and Unconventional English,* in effect a supplement to *The Oxford English Dictionary,* whose editors puritanically and unwisely omitted many terms that are to be found not only among speakers of the language but also in books of imaginative literature.

Foreign-language dictionaries are necessary for readers of other literatures; some of the best are listed in the main body of the present compilation.

Two goldmines of another sort are *The Oxford Companion to American Literature* and *The Oxford Companion to English Literature.* These are ready-reference volumes, alphabetically arranged lists of allusions (Grub Street, Peeping Tom, the Wandering Jew), identification of classical and other references (Artemis, Orator Henley, Meleager), brief biographies of authors major and minor, characters in literary works, summaries of plots, and so forth. *The Oxford Companion to English Literature* even has wonderfully useful appendices, including a perpetual calendar and a table of saints' days (for instance Lady Day, often encountered in English literature, because as a so-called quarter day rents fell due then). No scholar would cite one of these companions as authority for a fact he wished to put forward (though these two volumes represent an extremely high level of accuracy), but every reader finds them altogether handy. Similar compilations are listed in the following pages, and their inclusion in *A Reader's Guide* constitutes an endorsement in terms like those in which the Oxford works are commended.

Every reader needs to have access to at least one encyclopedia. I use two, the one-volume *Columbia Encyclopedia,* which is excellent for its limited purpose; and *The Encyclopaedia Britannica*. Of the latter it should be said that the 11th edition, published in 1910–1911, is absolutely first-class. In fact it is superior in many respects to the more recent editions, which in appealing to a wider audience have become more "popular" (as well as more expensive). The 11th edition is still readily available in the second-hand bookshops—I saw a set in fine condition recently in Santa Barbara for $35.00.

Such are the utensils I recommend as the minimum desirable for the personal libraries of readers of literature. Many others are convenient and useful, and one of the purposes of the following pages is to show the way to such larger possibilities—such as Robert Graves' splendid retelling of the Greek myths in two inexpensive paperbound volumes, and Harvey Gross' superb collection of essays on prosody, *The Structure of Verse*, also available in an inexpensive paperbound edition. But the *batterie de bibliothèque* in this introduction will enable the reader to begin to comprehend the works of literature with which he becomes engaged.

The only postscript that may be useful here has to do with how to write footnotes and how to make bibliographies. A brief pamphlet does this job of instruction briskly and authoritatively. It is *The MLA Style Sheet*—the initials stand for the Modern Language Association of America, which publishes the pamphlet and which has persuaded a large number of scholarly journals to agree to the practices set forth in it. Though *The MLA Style Sheet* does not offer a solution to every problem that may come up, its instructions are so clear and precise as to form a groundwork for the settlement of every stylistic issue that may arise.

English Literature

General

GUIDES TO LITERARY STUDY

ALTICK, RICHARD D. *The Art of Literary Research*. New York, 1963.
A distinguished American scholar's authoritative treatment, with fascinating examples, of what is involved in research.

ALTICK, RICHARD D., and ANDREW WRIGHT. *Selective Bibliography for the Study of English and American Literature*. 3rd ed. New York, 1967.
The standard "key to keys," this is a guide to books about literature and to the tools of research.

BATESON, F. W., et al. *The Cambridge Bibliography of English Literature*. 4 vols. Cambridge, 1940. Volume V (Supplement), ed. George Watson. Cambridge, 1957.
Generally referred to as "CBEL," this monumental work covers British authors from the beginnings of English literary history to 1900. The bibliographies are not exhaustive, and vary in quality. The one-volume condensation (2nd ed., Cambridge, 1965) is useful but spotty. CBEL can be supplemented by the "MLA International Bibliography," published annually in *PMLA* ("Publications of the Modern Language Association of America"). A revision of CBEL, under the editorship of George Watson, is in progress. The first volume issued (1969) covers the nineteenth century.

BATESON, F. W. *A Guide to English Literature*. 2nd ed. Garden City, New York, 1967.
A highly individual, not to say idiosyncratic, guide to literature itself, rather than to works about literature, though the latter are not scamped.

BOND, DONALD F. *A Reference Guide to English Studies*. Chicago, 1962.
Too extensive for all but the most advanced and indomitable students.

DAICHES, DAVID. *English Literature*. Englewood Cliffs, New Jersey, 1964.
An account of the scope, methods, and fashions of literary study by an erudite Scottish scholar educated in England with long experience in the U.S.A. (at Chicago and Cornell).

SERIAL GUIDES TO LITERARY STUDY

"MLA International Bibliography of Books and Articles on the Modern Languages and Literatures." *PMLA*, 1922–   .
The best and most comprehensive annually produced bibliog-

raphy, issued as part of the membership in the Modern Language Association of America, to which all scholars ought to belong as a matter of course. Previous to issue for 1956, included books and articles by American scholars only.

ENGLISH ASSOCIATION. *The Year's Work in English Studies.* (1919–   .) London, 1921–   .

Selective, critical, discursive, uneven.

Studies in English Literature, 1500–1900. 1961–   .

Each quarterly issue contains a bibliographically invaluable survey of recent scholarship in one of the following fields: The English Renaissance (Winter), Elizabethan and Jacobean Drama (Spring), Restoration and Eighteenth Century (Summer), Nineteenth Century (Autumn).

REFERENCE WORKS

Annals of English Literature, 1475–1950, ed. J. C. GHOSH. 2nd ed., revised by R. W. Chapman and Winifred Davin. Oxford, 1961.

A chronology of "the principal publications of each year" together with events pertinent to literary history.

BENÉT, WILLIAM ROSE. *The Reader's Encyclopedia.* 2nd ed. New York, 1965.

A wide-ranging and necessarily superficial catch-all in a single alphabetical arrangement.

Dictionary of National Biography, ed. LESLIE STEPHEN and SIDNEY LEE. 63 vols. London, 1885–1900.

Later reissued in 21 volumes. Fine as a first—or as a desperate last—resort, but now inevitably dated, although supplements and lists of errata continue to be published. Two epitome volumes, called *The Concise Dictionary* and extending through 1950, were issued in 1953 and 1961.

GRAVES, ROBERT. *The Greek Myths.* 2 vols. London, 1955.

A lucid retelling of the principal myths.

GROSS, HARVEY, ed. *The Structure of Verse: Modern Essays on Prosody.* Greenwich, Connecticut, 1966.

Essays by a number of distinguished prosodists including Otto Jespersen, Robert Graves, Wimsatt and Beardsley, and Northrop Frye, together with appendices on meter, rhyme, and the terminology of prosody.

LANHAM, RICHARD A. *A Handlist of Rhetorical Terms.* Berkeley, 1968.

The MLA Style Sheet, compiled by JOHN HURT FISHER et al. 2nd ed. New York, 1970.

No student of literature should be without this pamphlet devoted to scholarly style—that is, how to make footnotes and bibliographies.

The Oxford Companion to English Literature, ed. PAUL HARVEY. 4th ed. Oxford, 1967.

A resolutely old-fashioned and deliberately tame compilation containing information in a single alphabetical list about authors, literary characters, forms, and including brief plot summaries.

The Oxford English Dictionary, ed. JAMES A. H. MURRAY et al. 13 vols. Oxford, 1933.

Originally issued (1888–1928) as *A New English Dictionary on Historical Principles,* this splendid dictionary is absolutely indispensable to the reader of English literature, although the abridgment, *The Shorter Oxford English Dictionary* (3rd ed., Oxford, 1955) is useful as well.

PARTRIDGE, ERIC. *A Dictionary of Slang and Unconventional English.* 5th ed. 2 vols. London, 1961.

PREMINGER, ALEX, et al. *Encyclopedia of Poetry and Poetics.* Princeton, 1965.

Far more comprehensive than the title indicates, and absolutely first-class.

LITERARY HISTORY

BAUGH, ALBERT C., et al. *A Literary History of England.* 2nd ed. New York, 1967.

Also published in four parts. Comprehensive, dependable, sometimes brilliant, occasionally dauntingly fact-laden.

CRAIG, HARDIN, et al. *A History of English Literature.* New York, 1950.

Also published, somewhat revised, in four parts (1962). Shorter and more readable but also more sketchy than the Baugh volume.

FORD, BORIS, ed. *The Pelican Guide to English Literature.* 7 vols. London, 1954–1961.

Uneven but sometimes exciting essays by the followers of the renowned antihistorical moralist, F. R. Leavis.

LEGOUIS, ÉMILE, and LOUIS CAZAMIAN. *A History of English Literature.* Revised ed. London, 1954.

Originally published in 1926–1927, this is old-fashioned but beautifully lucid and categorical.

The Oxford History of English Literature, ed. F. P. Wilson et al. Oxford, 1945– .

Of the fourteen projected volumes, ten have been published to date. Two or three of these volumes, listed under the appropriate period headings below, are the best studies available.

POLITICAL, SOCIAL, AND INTELLECTUAL HISTORY

The Oxford History of England, ed. Sir George Clark. 15 vols. Oxford, 1934–1965.

Standard and up-to-date. These volumes are listed under the appropriate period headings below.

Steinberg, S. H., ed. *A New Dictionary of British History.* New York, 1963.

A handbook omitting all purely biographical matter. An excellent source of information about such matters as "Agincourt," "Conventicle Act," "Plymouth Brethren."

Trevelyan, G. M. *History of England.* 3rd ed. London, 1945.

The best one-volume history, now available in three paperbound parts.

———. *Illustrated English Social History.* 4 vols. London, 1949–1952.

LANGUAGE

Baugh, Albert C. *A History of the English Language.* 2nd ed. New York, 1957.

Standard.

Bloomfield, Leonard. *Language.* New York, 1933.

The pioneering work in the re-study of language.

Bloomfield, Morton W., and Leonard Newmark. *A Linguistic Introduction to the History of English.* New York, 1965.

Chomsky, Noam. *Aspects of the Theory of Syntax.* Cambridge, Massachusetts, 1965.

See Chapter One especially.

Robins, R. H. *A Short History of Linguistics.* London, 1968.

Records the recent revolutions and fashions in linguistics.

FOLKLORE

Funk & Wagnalls Standard Dictionary of Folklore, Mythology and Legend, ed. Maria Leach and Jerome Fried. 2 vols. New York, 1949–1950.

Comprehensive and convenient to use.

THOMPSON, STITH. *The Folktale.* New York, 1946.
———. *Motif-Index of Folk-Literature.* Revised ed. 6 vols. Bloomington, 1955–1958.

POETRY

COURTHOPE, W. J. *A History of English Poetry.* 6 vols. London, 1895–1910.
Old-fashioned but comprehensive.
PREMINGER, ALEX, et al. *Encyclopedia of Poetry and Poetics.* Princeton, 1965.
Far more comprehensive than the title indicates, and absolutely first-class.
SAINTSBURY, GEORGE. *A History of English Prosody.* 3 vols. London, 1906–1910.
Dated but not obsolete.

DRAMA

HARBAGE, ALFRED. *Annals of English Drama, 975–1700.* Revised ed. by Samuel Schoenbaum. Philadelphia, 1964.
NICOLL, ALLARDYCE. *British Drama: An Historical Survey from the Beginnings to the Present Time.* 5th ed. New York, 1962.
The standard one-volume survey despite or because of its oversimplifications.
———. *A History of English Drama, 1660–1900.* 6 vols. Cambridge, 1952–1959.
Exhaustive but critically naive.
The Oxford Companion to the Theatre, ed. PHYLLIS HARTNOLL. 3rd ed. Oxford, 1967.
Covers the theatre "in all ages and in all countries" but excludes the cinema.

FICTION

ALLEN, WALTER. *The English Novel: A Short Critical History.* London, 1954.
Covers fewer authors—and novels—than does Stevenson's history, but is occasionally more interesting in its judgments.
BAKER, ERNEST A. *The History of the English Novel.* 10 vols. London, 1924–1939. Volume XI, by Lionel Stevenson. New York, 1967.
Lengthy, opinionated, inaccurate. The supplementary volume suffers, however, from none of the defects of the original.

STEVENSON, LIONEL. *The English Novel: A Panorama.* Boston, 1960.
   Panoramic indeed, and thorough.

CRITICISM

SAINTSBURY, GEORGE. *A History of English Criticism.* Edinburgh, 1911.
   Old-fashioned but lively and useful.
WATSON, GEORGE. *The Literary Critics.* London, 1962.
   Concise and lucid.
WIMSATT, WILLIAM K., JR., and CLEANTH BROOKS. *Literary Criticism: A Short History.* New York, 1957.
   Controversial because one-sided.

The Old English Period (to 1150)

BIBLIOGRAPHY

BONSER, WILFRID. *An Anglo-Saxon and Celtic Bibliography (450–1087)*. 2 vols. Berkeley, 1957.
Excludes "all material dealing with literature and linguistics as such."

MATTHEWS, WILLIAM. *Old and Middle English Literature*. New York, 1968.
A distinguished bibliography of "English literature and culture before 1525."

ZESMER, DAVID M. *Guide to English Literature from Beowulf Through Chaucer and Medieval Drama*. New York, 1961.
A survey, elementary but useful, together with an annotated bibliography.

LITERARY HISTORY

ANDERSON, GEORGE K. *The Literature of the Anglo-Saxons*. Princeton, 1949.

CHAMBERS, R. W. *On the Continuity of English Prose*. London, 1932.

GREENFIELD, STANLEY B. *A Critical History of Old English Literature*. New York, 1965.
Solid, economical, comprehensive, up-to-date.

KENNEDY, CHARLES W. *The Earliest English Poetry*. New York, 1943.

POLITICAL, SOCIAL, AND INTELLECTUAL HISTORY

ACKERMAN, ROBERT W. *Backgrounds to Medieval English Literature*. New York, 1966.
A study of the religious, philosophical, social, and linguistic atmosphere.

STENTON, F. M. *Anglo-Saxon England, c. 550–1087*. (*Oxford History of England,* vol. II.) 2nd ed. Oxford, 1947.
Standard and authoritative.

WHITELOCK, DOROTHY. *The Beginnings of English Society*. London, 1952.
A brief and highly regarded work.

EDITIONS

CLARK HALL, JOHN R. *Beowulf and the Finnsburg Fragment.* Revised
    by C. L. Wrenn. London, 1950.
    A prose version, generally thought to be the best translation
    available.
COOK, A. S., and C. B. TINKER. *Select Translations from Old English
    Prose.* Boston, 1908.
GORDON, R. K. *Anglo-Saxon Poetry.* Revised ed. New York, 1954.
    Prose translations.
KENNEDY, CHARLES W. *An Anthology of Old English Poetry.* New
    York, 1960.
    Contains translations in verse of *The Wanderer* and *The Sea-
    farer,* among others.
RAFFEL, BURTON. *Poems from the Old English.* 2nd ed. Lincoln,
    Nebraska, 1964.
SHERLEY PRICE, LEE. *A History of the English Church and People.*
    London, 1955.
    A translation of Bede's *Ecclesiastical History.*
WHITELOCK, DOROTHY, et al. *The Anglo-Saxon Chronicle.* New
    Brunswick, New Jersey, 1962.

BIOGRAPHY AND CRITICISM

BRODEUR, ARTHUR G. *The Art of Beowulf.* Berkeley, 1959.
CHAMBERS, R. W. *Beowulf: An Introduction.* With a Supplement by
    C. L. Wrenn. 3rd ed. Cambridge, 1959.
FRY, DONALD K., ed. *The Beowulf Poet.* Englewood Cliffs, New
    Jersey, 1968.
    Essays by various critics.
IRVING, EDWARD B., JR. *A Reading of Beowulf.* New Haven, 1968.
KER, W. P. *Epic and Romance.* 2nd ed. London, 1908.
NICHOLSON, LEWIS E., ed. *An Anthology of Beowulf Criticism.*
    Notre Dame, Indiana, 1963.
SISAM, KENNETH. *The Structure of Beowulf.* Oxford, 1965.
THOMPSON, A. HAMILTON, ed. *Bede: His Life, Times, and Writings.*
    Oxford, 1935.
WHITELOCK, DOROTHY. *The Audience of Beowulf.* Oxford, 1951.

The Middle English Period (1150–1500)

BIBLIOGRAPHY

MATTHEWS, WILLIAM. *Old and Middle English Literature.* New York, 1968.
A distinguished bibliography of "English literature and culture before 1525."

WELLS, JOHN E. *A Manual of the Writings in Middle English, 1050–1400.* New Haven, 1916. Supplements. 9 vols. New Haven, 1919–1952.
Maddeningly complicated to use. For many purposes the first volume of the *Cambridge Bibliography of English Literature* is adequate, and much more convenient than Wells. A revision, edited by J. B. Severs, is imminent.

LITERARY HISTORY

BENNETT, H. S. *Chaucer and the Fifteenth Century.* (*Oxford History of English Literature,* vol. II, part 1.) Oxford, 1947.

CHAMBERS, E. K. *English Literature at the Close of the Middle Ages.* (*Oxford History of English Literature,* vol. II, part 2.) Oxford, 1945.

CHAMBERS, R. W. *On the Continuity of English Prose.* Oxford, 1957.

KANE, GEORGE. *Middle English Literature: A Critical Study of the Romances, the Religious Lyrics, Piers Plowman.* London, 1951.

KER, W. P. *English Literature Mediaeval,* London, 1912.
Recent reprints are titled *Medieval English Literature.*

LEWIS, C. S. *The Allegory of Love: A Study in Medieval Tradition.* Revised ed. London, 1938.
Controversial, racy, readable.

LOOMIS, ROGER SHERMAN, ed. *Arthurian Literature in the Middle Ages.* Oxford, 1959.

SCHLAUCH, MARGARET. *English Medieval Literature and Its Social Foundations.* Warsaw, 1956.
A brilliant treatment by a Marxist medievalist.

SPEIRS, JOHN. *Medieval English Poetry: The Non-Chaucerian Tradition.* London, 1957.

WILSON, R. M. *Early Middle English Literature.* 2nd ed. London, 1951.

POLITICAL, SOCIAL, AND INTELLECTUAL HISTORY

COULTON, G. G. *Medieval Panorama.* Cambridge, 1938.
A survey, by topics, of medieval civilization.

HUIZINGA, JOHAN. *The Waning of the Middle Ages.* London, 1924.
A brilliant study of medieval ideas, including chivalry, social classes, symbolism, and death.

JACOB, ERNEST F. *The Fifteenth Century, 1399–1485. (Oxford History of England, vol. VI.)* Oxford, 1961.

MCKISACK, MAY. *The Fourteenth Century, 1307–1399. (Oxford History of England, vol. V.)* Oxford, 1951.

MYERS, A. R. *England in the Late Middle Ages.* London, 1952.

POOLE, A. L. *From Domesday Book to Magna Carta, 1087–1216. (Oxford History of England, vol. III.)* 2nd ed. Oxford, 1955.

POWICKE, Sir MAURICE. *The Thirteenth Century, 1216–1307. (Oxford History of England, vol. IV.)* 2nd ed. London, 1962.

STENTON, D. M. *English Society in the Middle Ages (1066–1307).* 2nd ed. London, 1959.

COLLECTIONS

ADAMS, JOSEPH Q. *Chief Pre-Shakespearean Dramas.* Boston, 1924.
A usefully inclusive and annotated anthology.

CAWLEY, A. C. *Everyman and Medieval Miracle Plays.* London, 1956.

CHAMBERS, E. K., and F. SIDGWICK. *Early English Lyrics.* London, 1907.

DAVIES, R. T. *Medieval English Lyrics.* Evanston, Illinois, 1963.
An anthology, including translations where necessary.

GIBBS, A. C. *Middle English Romances.* Evanston, Illinois, 1966.

LOOMIS, ROGER SHERMAN, and RUDOLPH WILLARD. *Medieval English Verse and Prose.* New York, 1948.

SCHELL, EDGAR T., and J. D. SHUCHTER. *English Morality Plays and Moral Interludes.* New York, 1969.
Ranges from the fourteenth-century *Castle of Perseverance* through *The Conflict of Conscience* (1581).

SISAM, KENNETH, ed. *Fourteenth Century Verse and Prose.* Oxford, 1921.

STEVICK, ROBERT D. *One Hundred Middle English Lyrics.* Indianapolis, 1964.

BALLADS

CHILD, FRANCIS J. *The English and Scottish Popular Ballads.* 5 vols. Boston, 1883–1898.
   The classic compilation, now available in a paperbound edition.
FRIEDMAN, ALBERT B. *The Viking Book of Folk Ballads.* New York, 1956.
   A good selection.
GEROULD, GORDON HALL. *The Ballad of Tradition.* Oxford, 1932.
   A book of criticism.
GRAVES, ROBERT. *English and Scottish Ballads.* London, 1957.
   A good selection.
HODGART, M. J. C. *The Ballads.* London, 1950.
   A brief introduction.
WELLS, EVELYN KENDRICK. *The Ballad Tree.* New York, 1950.
   A book of criticism plus a collection of ballads and tunes.

DRAMA

CHAMBERS, E. K. *The Mediaeval Stage.* 2 vols. Oxford, 1903.
   Monumental and comprehensive.
HARDISON, O. B. *Christian Rite and Christian Drama in the Middle Ages.* Baltimore, 1965.
KOLVE, V. A. *The Play Called Corpus Christi.* Stanford, California, 1966.
YOUNG, KARL. *The Drama of the Medieval Church.* 2 vols. Oxford, 1933.

SIR GAWAIN AND THE GREEN KNIGHT

Editions

ROSENBERG, JAMES L. *Sir Gawain and the Green Knight.* New York, 1959.
   A translation.
TOLKIEN, J. R. R., and E. V. GORDON. *Sir Gawain and the Green Knight.* 2nd ed. Oxford, 1967.
   Includes notes and glossary.

Criticism

BLANCH, ROBERT J., ed. *Sir Gawain and Pearl: Critical Essays.* Bloomington, Indiana, 1966.
   Essays by various critics.

BOROFF, MARIE. *Sir Gawain and the Green Knight*. New Haven, 1962.

HOWARD, DONALD R., and C. K. ZACHER, eds. *Critical Studies of Sir Gawain and the Green Knight*. Notre Dame, Indiana, 1968. Essays by various critics.

JOHN GOWER (ca. 1330–1408)

Editions

BENNETT, J. A. W. *Selections*. New York, 1968.

MACAULAY, GEORGE C. *Complete Works*. 4 vols. Oxford, 1899–1902.

TILLER, TERENCE. *Confessio Amantis*. London, 1963. A modernized version.

Biography and Criticism

FISHER, JOHN H. *John Gower*. New York, 1964.

WILLIAM LANGLAND (ca. 1332–ca. 1400)

Editions

GOODRIDGE, J. F. *Langland: Piers the Plowman*. London, 1959. A prose translation of the B-text.

KANE, GEORGE. *Piers Plowman: The A Version*. Oxford, 1960.

Criticism

DONALDSON, E. TALBOT. *Piers Plowman: The C-Text and Its Poet*. New Haven, 1949. More comprehensive than its title suggests.

FRANK, ROBERT W., JR. *Piers Plowman and the Scheme of Salvation*. New Haven, 1957.

GEOFFREY CHAUCER (ca. 1343–1400)

Editions

COGHILL, NEVILL. *The Canterbury Tales Translated into Modern English*. London, 1952.

DONALDSON, E. TALBOT. *Chaucer's Poetry: An Anthology for the Modern Reader*. New York, 1958. Well edited and arranged.

MANLY, JOHN M., and EDITH RICKERT. *The Text of the Canterbury Tales.* 8 vols. Chicago, 1940.
>Authoritative but difficult to use. Not for the beginner.

ROBINSON, F. N. *The Works of Geoffrey Chaucer.* 2nd ed. Boston, 1957.
>The standard edition of the full corpus.

Guides

BAUGH, ALBERT C. *Chaucer.* New York, 1968.
>A fine and up-to-date bibliography.

FRENCH, ROBERT D. *A Chaucer Handbook.* 2nd ed. New York, 1947.
>A collection of materials for biographical and critical judgment.

ROWLAND, BERYL, ed. *A Companion to Chaucer Studies.* New York, 1968.

Biography

CHUTE, MARCHETTE. *Geoffrey Chaucer of England.* New York, 1946.

Criticism

BREWER, D. S. *Chaucer in His Time.* London, 1963.

KITTREDGE, GEORGE LYMAN. *Chaucer and His Poetry.* Cambridge, Massachusetts, 1915.
>Old-fashioned but stimulating.

LAWRENCE, WILLIAM W. *Chaucer and the Canterbury Tales.* London, 1950.

LOWES, JOHN LIVINGSTON. *Geoffrey Chaucer.* London, 1934.

LUMIANSKY, R. M. *Of Sondry Folk: The Dramatic Principle in the Canterbury Tales.* Austin, Texas, 1955.

MUSCATINE, CHARLES. *Chaucer and the French Tradition: A Study in Style and Meaning.* Berkeley, 1957.
>Ranges further than its title suggests.

ROBERTSON, D. W. *A Preface to Chaucer.* Princeton, 1963.

ROOT, ROBERT K. *The Poetry of Chaucer.* 2nd ed. New York, 1922.

RUGGIERS, PAUL G. *The Art of the Canterbury Tales.* Madison, Wisconsin, 1965.

WAGENKNECHT, EDWARD, ed. *Chaucer: Modern Essays in Criticism.* New York, 1959.
>Essays by various critics.

WHITTOCK, TREVOR. *A Reading of the Canterbury Tales*. London, 1968.

SIR THOMAS MALORY (d. 1471)

Editions

VINAVER, EUGÈNE. *Works*. 3 vols. Oxford, 1947.
　　The text, minus much apparatus, was published in one volume in 1954, and a second edition was issued in 1969.
――――. *King Arthur and His Knights*. Boston, 1956.
　　A judicious selection.

Criticism

BENNETT, J. A. W., ed. *Essays on Malory*. Oxford, 1963.
　　Essays by various Malory scholars.
LUMIANSKY, R. M., ed. *Malory's Originality*. Baltimore, 1964.
　　Also a collection of essays by several hands.
MATTHEWS, WILLIAM. *The Ill-Framed Knight*. Berkeley, 1966.

The Sixteenth Century

BIBLIOGRAPHY

LIEVSAY, JOHN L. *The Sixteenth Century: Skelton Through Hooker.* New York, 1968.

"Literature of the Renaissance." Annually in *Studies in Philology,* 1917– .

RIBNER, IRVING. *Tudor and Stuart Drama.* New York, 1966.
An excellent comprehensive guide.

LITERARY HISTORY

ALPERS, PAUL J., ed. *Elizabethan Poetry.* New York, 1967.
Essays by various critics.

BOAS, FREDERICK S. *An Introduction to Tudor Drama.* Oxford, 1933.

BRADBROOK, M. C. *The Growth and Structure of Elizabethan Comedy.* London, 1955.

———. *Themes and Conventions of Elizabethan Tragedy.* Cambridge, 1935.

CHAMBERS, E. K. *The Elizabethan Stage.* 4 vols. Oxford, 1923.
The standard work.

GRUNDY, JOAN. *The Spenserian Poets: A Study in Elizabethan and Jacobean Poetry.* London, 1969.
Treats Michael Drayton, George Wither, William Browne, Giles and Phineas Fletcher.

KAUFMANN, RALPH J., ed. *Elizabethan Drama.* New York, 1961.
Essays by various critics.

LEWIS, C. S. *English Literature in the Sixteenth Century, Excluding Drama. (Oxford History of English Literature,* vol. III.) Oxford, 1954.
Controversial but readable.

MUIR, KENNETH. *An Introduction to Elizabethan Literature.* New York, 1967.
Concentrates on the major figures.

WILSON, F. P. *The English Drama, 1485–1585. (Oxford History of English Literature,* vol. IV, part 1.) Oxford, 1969.

POLITICAL, SOCIAL, AND INTELLECTUAL HISTORY

BLACK, J. B. *The Reign of Elizabeth, 1558–1603. (Oxford History of England,* vol. VIII.) 2nd ed. Oxford, 1959.

BOLGAR, R. R. *The Classical Heritage and Its Beneficiaries.* Cambridge, 1954.

Very highly regarded.

CASPARI, FRITZ. *Humanism and the Social Order in Tudor England.* Chicago, 1954.

MACKIE, J. D. *The Earlier Tudors, 1485–1558.* (*Oxford History of England,* vol. VII.) Oxford, 1952.

TILLYARD, E. M. W. *The Elizabethan World Picture.* London, 1943.

COLLECTIONS

ADAMS, JOSEPH Q. *Chief Pre-Shakespearian Dramas.* Boston, 1924.

A usefully inclusive and annotated anthology.

AULT, NORMAN. *Elizabethan Lyrics.* 3rd ed. New York, 1949.

BASKERVILL, C. R., et al. *Elizabethan and Stuart Plays.* New York, 1934.

Contains forty-two plays.

BULLETT, GERALD. *Silver Poets of the Sixteenth Century.* New York, 1947.

CREETH, EDMUND. *Tudor Plays.* Garden City, New York, 1966.

HEBEL, J. WILLIAM, and HOYT H. HUDSON. *Poetry of the English Renaissance, 1509–1660.* New York, 1929.

A standard and generously representative anthology.

LAWLIS, MERRITT. *Elizabethan Prose Fiction.* New York, 1968.

Contains nine works.

McCLURE, NORMAN E. *Sixteenth-Century English Poetry.* New York, 1954.

ORNSTEIN, ROBERT, and HAZLETON SPENCER. *Elizabethan and Jacobean Comedy.* Boston, 1964.

———. *Elizabethan and Jacobean Tragedy.* Boston, 1964.

SAINTSBURY, GEORGE. *Shorter Elizabethan Novels.* London, 1929.

Jack of Newberie and *Thomas of Reading* by Thomas Deloney, *Cards of Fancie* by Robert Greene, *The Unfortunate Traveller* by Thomas Nashe.

TOTTEL, RICHARD. *Songes and Sonettes,* ed. Hyder E. Rollins. 2 vols. Cambridge, Massachusetts, 1928–1929.

Better known as Tottel's *Miscellany.*

JOHN SKELTON (ca. 1460–1529)

Editions

DE SOLA PINTO, VIVIAN. *A Selection.* London, 1950.

HENDERSON, PHILIP. *Complete Poems.* 2nd ed. London, 1948.

Biography and Criticism

EDWARDS, H. L. R. *Skelton: The Life and Times of an Early Tudor Poet*. London, 1949.

FISH, STANLEY EUGENE. *John Skelton's Poetry*. New Haven, 1965.

GORDON, IAN A. *John Skelton: Poet Laureate*. Melbourne, 1943.

HEISERMAN, A. R. *Skelton and Satire*. Chicago, 1961.

NELSON, WILLIAM. *John Skelton: Laureate*. New York, 1939.

SIR THOMAS MORE (1478–1535)

Editions

OGDEN, H. V. S. *Utopia*. New York, 1949.
A modern translation.

ROGERS, ELIZABETH F. *Correspondence*. Princeton, 1947.

SYLVESTER, RICHARD S. *Complete Works*. New Haven, 1963–
In progress.

Biography

CHAMBERS, R. W. *Thomas More*. New York, 1935.

Criticism

AMES, RUSSELL. *Citizen Thomas More and His Utopia*. Princeton, 1949.

DONNER, H. W. *Introduction to Utopia*. London, 1945.

HEXTER, JACK H. *More's Utopia: The Biography of an Idea*. Princeton, 1952.

NELSON, WILLIAM, ed. *Twentieth-Century Interpretations of Utopia*. Englewood Cliffs, New Jersey, 1968.
Essays by various critics.

SIR THOMAS WYATT (1503–1542)

Edition

MUIR, KENNETH. *Collected Poems*. London, 1949.

Biography and Criticism

MUIR, KENNETH. *Life and Letters*. Liverpool, 1963.

SOUTHALL, R. *The Courtly Maker*. New York, 1964.

THOMSON, PATRICIA. *Sir Thomas Wyatt and His Background*. Stanford, California, 1964.

ROGER ASCHAM (1515–1568)

Edition

WRIGHT, W. ALDIS. *English Works*. Cambridge, 1904.

Biography and Criticism

RYAN, LAWRENCE V. *Roger Ascham*. Stanford, California, 1963.

HENRY HOWARD, EARL OF SURREY (1517–1547)

Editions

JONES, EMRYS. *Poems*. Oxford, 1964.
PADELFORD, F. M. *Poems*. Revised ed. Seattle, 1928.

Biography

CASADY, EDWIN. *Henry Howard, Earl of Surrey*. New York, 1938.

GEORGE GASCOIGNE (ca. 1525–1577)

Editions

CUNLIFFE, J. W. *Complete Works*. 2 vols. Cambridge, 1907–1910.
PROUTY, C. T. *A Hundreth Sundrie Flowres*. Columbia, Missouri, 1942.

Biography and Criticism

PROUTY, C. T. *George Gascoigne*. New York, 1942.

THOMAS DELONEY (ca. 1543–ca. 1600)

Editions

LAWLIS, MERRITT E. *Novels*. Bloomington, Indiana, 1961.
MANN, F. O. *Works*. Oxford, 1912.
  Reissued in 1967.

Criticism

LAWLIS, MERRITT E. *Apology for the Middle Class: The Dramatic Novels of Thomas Deloney*. Bloomington, Indiana, 1960.

SIR WALTER RALEGH (ca. 1552–1618)

Editions

LATHAM, AGNES M. C. *Poems.* Revised ed. Cambridge, Massachusetts, 1951.
———. *Selected Prose and Poetry.* London, 1965.

Biography and Criticism

BRADBROOK, M. C. *The School of Night.* Cambridge, 1936.
EDWARDS, PHILIP. *Sir Walter Ralegh.* London, 1953.
STRATHMANN, ERNEST A. *Sir Walter Ralegh.* New York, 1951.

EDMUND SPENSER (1552–1599)

Editions

GREENLAW, EDWIN, et al. *Works.* 9 vols. Baltimore, 1932–1949. Index. Baltimore, 1957.
   The standard edition, a variorum. Cumbersome, pedantic, of uneven quality. Now being revised.
KELLOGG, ROBERT L., and OLIVER L. STEELE. *The Faerie Queene.* New York, 1967.
   Contains Books I and II, the Mutability Cantos, and a number of the minor poems in modernized, well-annotated versions.
SMITH, J. C., and E. DE SELINCOURT. *Poetical Works.* Oxford, 1912.
   A convenient one-volume edition.

Biography

JUDSON, ALEXANDER C. *The Life of Edmund Spenser.* Baltimore, 1945.
   In the Greenlaw edition of the *Works,* listed above.

Criticism

ALPERS, PAUL J. *The Poetry of The Faerie Queene,* Princeton, 1967.
BERGER, HARRY, JR., ed. *Spenser: A Collection of Critical Essays.* Englewood Cliffs, New Jersey, 1968.
   Essays by various critics.
DAVIS, B. E. C. *Edmund Spenser: A Critical Study.* Cambridge, 1933.
DUNSEATH, THOMAS K. *Spenser's Allegory of Justice.* Princeton, 1968.

FOWLER, ALASTAIR. *Spenser and the Numbers of Time*. New York, 1964.

HAMILTON, A. C. *The Structure of Allegory in The Faerie Queene*. Oxford, 1961.

HOUGH, GRAHAM. *A Preface to The Faerie Queene*. London, 1962.

JONES, H. S. V. *A Spenser Handbook*. New York, 1930.
  Contains much useful information.

NELSON, WILLIAM. *The Poetry of Edmund Spenser*. New York, 1963.

ROSE, MARK. *Heroic Love: Studies in Sidney and Spenser*. Cambridge, Massachusetts, 1968.

SALE, ROGER. *Reading Spenser: An Introduction to The Faerie Queene*. New York, 1968.

RICHARD HAKLUYT (ca. 1553–1616)

Edition

MASEFIELD, JOHN. *The Principal Navigations*. 10 vols. London, 1927–1928.

Biography and Criticism

PARKS, GEORGE B. *Richard Hakluyt and the English Voyages*. New York, 1928.

FULKE GREVILLE, LORD BROOKE (1554–1628)

Editions

BULLOUGH, GEOFFREY. *Poems and Dramas*. 2 vols. Edinburgh, 1939.

GUNN, THOM. *Selected Poems*. London, 1968.

JOHN LYLY (ca. 1554–1606)

Editions

BOND, R. WARWICK. *Complete Works*. 3 vols. Oxford, 1902.

WINNY, JAMES. *The Descent of Euphues: Three Elizabethan Romance Stories*. Cambridge, 1957.
  Includes *Euphues*.

Biography and Criticism

HUNTER, G. K. *John Lyly: The Humanist as Courtier*. Cambridge, Massachusetts, 1962.

SIR PHILIP SIDNEY (1554–1586)

Editions

FEUILLERAT, ALBERT. *The Prose Works.* 4 vols. Cambridge, 1912–1926.

KIMBROUGH, ROBERT. *Selected Prose and Poetry.* New York, 1969.

RINGLER, WILLIAM A. *Poems.* Oxford, 1962.

Biography

BOAS, FREDERICK S. *Sir Philip Sidney: Representative Elizabethan.* London, 1955.

BUXTON, JOHN. *Sir Philip Sidney and the English Renaissance.* 2nd ed. London, 1964.

WALLACE, MALCOLM W. *The Life of Sir Philip Sidney.* Cambridge, 1915.

WILSON, MONA. *Sir Philip Sidney.* London, 1931.

Criticism

KALSTONE, DAVID. *Sidney's Poetry.* Cambridge, Massachusetts, 1965.

MONTGOMERY, ROBERT. *Symmetry and Sense.* Austin, Texas, 1961.

MYRICK, K. O. *Sir Philip Sidney as a Literary Craftsman.* Cambridge, Massachusetts, 1935.

ROSE, MARK. *Heroic Love: Studies in Sidney and Spenser.* Cambridge, Massachusetts, 1968.

THOMAS KYD (1558–1594)

Edition

BOAS, FREDERICK S. *Works.* 2nd ed. Oxford, 1962.

Biography and Criticism

EDWARDS, PHILIP. *Thomas Kyd and Early Elizabethan Tragedy.* London, 1966.

FREEMAN, ARTHUR. *Thomas Kyd: Facts and Problems.* Oxford, 1967.

THOMAS LODGE (ca. 1558–1625)

Edition

GOSSE, EDMUND. *Complete Works.* 4 vols. Glasgow, 1883.

Biography and Criticism

PARADISE, N. BURTON. *Thomas Lodge*. New Haven, 1931.

GEORGE PEELE (ca. 1558–ca. 1597)

Edition

PROUTY, CHARLES TYLER, et al. *Life and Works*. 2 vols. New Haven, 1952–1961.

GEORGE CHAPMAN (ca. 1559–1634)

Editions

BARTLETT, PHYLLIS B. *Poems*. New York, 1941.
HOLADAY, ALLAN, et al. *The Plays: The Comedies*. Urbana, Illinois, 1969.
NICOLL, ALLARDYCE. *Chapman's Homer*. 2 vols. New York, 1956.
PARROTT, THOMAS MARC. *Plays and Poems*. 2 vols. New York, 1910, 1914.
The volume containing the poems was never published.

Biography and Criticism

MACLURE, MILLAR. *George Chapman: A Critical Study*. Toronto, 1966.
REES, ENNIS. *The Tragedies of George Chapman*. Cambridge, Massachusetts, 1954.
SPIVACK, CHARLOTTE. *George Chapman*. New York, 1967.

ROBERT GREENE (ca. 1560–1592)

Editions

CHURTON COLLINS, J. *Plays and Poems*. 2 vols. Oxford, 1905.
GROSART, ALEXANDER B. *Life and Complete Works*. 15 vols. London, 1881–1886.

ROBERT SOUTHWELL (1561–1595)

Edition

GROSART, A. B. *Complete Poems*. London, 1872.

Biography and Criticism

DEVLIN, CHRISTOPHER. *The Life of Robert Southwell: Poet and Martyr.* New York, 1956.

SAMUEL DANIEL (1562–1619)

Editions

GROSART, A. B. *Complete Works.* 5 vols. London, 1885–1896.
SPRAGUE, ARTHUR COLBY. *Poems, and a Defence of Ryme.* Cambridge, Massachusetts, 1930.

Biography and Criticism

REES, JOAN. *Samuel Daniel.* Liverpool, 1964.

MICHAEL DRAYTON (1563–1631)

Editions

BUXTON, JOHN. *Poems.* 2 vols. London, 1953.
HEBEL, J. WILLIAM, et al. *Complete Works.* 5 vols. Oxford, 1931–1941.

Biography and Criticism

NEWDIGATE, BERNARD H. *Michael Drayton and His Circle.* Oxford, 1941.

CHRISTOPHER MARLOWE (1564–1593)

Editions

CASE, R. H., et al. *Works.* 2nd ed. London, 1951– .
   The standard edition. The revision is in progress.
MacLURE, MILLAR. *Poems.* London, 1968.
RIBNER, IRVING. *Complete Plays.* New York, 1963.

Biography

BAKELESS, JOHN. *The Tragical History of Christopher Marlowe.* 2 vols. Cambridge, Massachusetts, 1942.
BOAS, F. S. *Christopher Marlowe: A Biographical and Critical Study.* 2nd ed. Oxford, 1953.

Criticism

KOCHER, PAUL H. *Christopher Marlowe.* Chapel Hill, North Carolina, 1946.

LEECH, CLIFFORD, ed. *Marlowe: A Collection of Critical Essays.* Englewood Cliffs, New Jersey, 1964.

Essays by various critics.

LEVIN, HARRY. *The Overreacher.* Cambridge, Massachusetts, 1952.

STEANE, J. B. *Marlowe.* Cambridge, 1964.

WILSON, F. P. *Marlowe and the Early Shakespeare.* Oxford, 1953.

WILLIAM SHAKESPEARE (1564–1616)

Guides

BERMAN, RONALD S. *A Reader's Guide to Shakespeare's Plays.* Chicago, 1965.

An extremely useful play-by-play guide to Shakespeare criticism.

CAMPBELL, OSCAR JAMES, and EDWARD G. QUINN. *The Reader's Encyclopedia of Shakespeare.* New York, 1966.

A gold mine.

HALLIDAY, F. E. *A Shakespeare Companion.* London, 1952.

Editions

ALEXANDER, PETER. *Complete Works.* 4 vols. London, 1934–1938.

CRAIG, HARDIN. *The Complete Works.* Chicago, 1951.

Well annotated.

ELLIS-FERMOR, UNA, et al. *The New Arden Shakespeare.* London, 1951– .

In progress.

HARRISON, G. B. *Major Plays and the Sonnets.* New York, 1948.

Well annotated.

KITTREDGE, GEORGE LYMAN. *Complete Works.* Boston, 1936.

Biography

ALEXANDER, PETER. *Shakespeare's Life and Art.* London, 1939.

CHAMBERS, E. K. *William Shakespeare.* 2 vols. Oxford, 1930.

Standard.

CHUTE, MARCHETTE. *Shakespeare of London.* New York, 1949.

Very readable.

Criticism

BRADLEY, A. C. *Shakespearean Tragedy.* 2nd ed. London, 1905.
A classic treatment, with which not everyone agrees. On *Hamlet, Othello, King Lear, Macbeth.*

BURCKHARDT, SIGURD. *Shakespearean Meanings.* Princeton, 1968.
Brilliant and controversial.

DEAN, LEONARD F., ed. *Shakespeare: Modern Essays in Criticism.* Revised ed. New York, 1967.
Essays by various critics.

GRANVILLE-BARKER, HARLEY. *Prefaces to Shakespeare.* 2 vols. Princeton, 1946–1947.
Written from the viewpoint of staging the plays.

HALLIDAY, F. E. *Shakespeare and His Critics.* London, 1949.
Considers various critical viewpoints; contains a selection of Shakespeare criticism.

SPURGEON, CAROLINE F. E. *Shakespeare's Imagery.* Cambridge, 1935.

STOLL, ELMER E. *Art and Artifice in Shakespeare.* New York, 1933.

TILLYARD, E. M. W. *Shakespeare's History Plays.* London, 1944.

WILSON KNIGHT, G. *The Wheel of Fire.* 2nd ed. Oxford, 1949.
First published in 1930, this is the most exciting of three studies of Shakespeare by Wilson Knight.

THOMAS CAMPION (1567–1620)

Edition

VIVIAN, PERCIVAL. *Works.* Oxford, 1909.

Biography and Criticism

KASTENDIECK, MILES M. *England's Musical Poet: Thomas Campion.* New York, 1938.

LOWBURY, EDWARD. *Thomas Campion.* London, 1969.

THOMAS NASHE (1567–1601)

Editions

MCKERROW, R. B. *Works.* 5 vols. London, 1904–1910.
A revised edition was issued in 1958.

WELLS, STANLEY. *Selected Writings.* Cambridge, Massachusetts, 1965.

Criticism

HIBBARD, G. R. *Thomas Nashe: A Critical Introduction.* Cambridge, Massachusetts, 1962.

THOMAS DEKKER (ca. 1570–1632)

Editions

BOWERS, FREDSON. *Dramatic Works.* 4 vols. Cambridge, 1953–1961.
McKERROW, R. B. *The Gull's Horn-Book.* London, 1904.

BEN JONSON (ca. 1573–1637)

Edition

HERFORD, C. H., and PERCY and EVELYN SIMPSON. *Works.* 11 vols. Oxford, 1925–1952.
Standard and indispensable.

Biography

CHUTE, MARCHETTE. *Ben Jonson of Westminster.* New York, 1953.
HERFORD, C. H., and PERCY SIMPSON. *Life of Jonson* (in *Works,* I, II). Oxford, 1925.

Criticism

BARISH, JONAS A. *Ben Jonson and the Language of Prose Comedy.* Cambridge, Massachusetts, 1960.
————, ed. *Ben Jonson: A Collection of Critical Essays.* Englewood Cliffs, New Jersey, 1963.
Essays by various critics.
PARTRIDGE, EDWARD B. *The Broken Compass: A Study of the Major Comedies of Ben Jonson.* New York, 1958.
TRIMPI, WESLEY. *Ben Jonson's Poems.* Stanford, California, 1962.

JOHN MARSTON (1576–1634)

Editions

DAVENPORT, ARNOLD. *Poems.* Liverpool, 1961.
WOOD, H. HARVEY. *Plays.* 3 vols. Edinburgh, 1934–1938.

Biography and Criticism

CAPUTI, ANTHONY. *John Marston, Satirist.* Ithaca, New York, 1961.

JOHN FLETCHER (1579–1625) and FRANCIS BEAUMONT (ca. 1585–1616)

Edition

GLOVER, ARNOLD, and A. R. WALLER. *Works* [of Beaumont and Fletcher]. 10 vols. Cambridge, 1905–1912. Being superseded by Fredson Bowers' edition of *The Dramatic Works,* Cambridge, 1966–   .

Biography and Criticism

APPLETON, WILLIAM W. *Beaumont and Fletcher.* London, 1956.
LEECH, CLIFFORD. *The John Fletcher Plays.* London, 1962.
WAITH, EUGENE M. *The Pattern of Tragicomedy in Beaumont and Fletcher.* New Haven, 1952.

JOHN WEBSTER (ca. 1580–ca. 1625)

Edition

LUCAS, F. L. *Works.* 4 vols. London, 1927.

Biography and Criticism

BOGARD, TRAVIS. *The Tragic Satire of John Webster.* Berkeley, 1955.
LEECH, CLIFFORD. *John Webster: A Critical Study.* London, 1951.

PHILIP MASSINGER (1583–1648)

Edition

SYMONS, ARTHUR. *Philip Massinger.* 2 vols. London, 1904.
Ten plays.

Biography and Criticism

DUNN, THOMAS A. *Philip Massinger.* Edinburgh, 1957.
LAWLESS, DONALD S. *Philip Massinger and His Associates.* Muncie, Indiana, 1967.

THE MADRIGAL

BOYD, M. C. *Elizabethan Music and Musical Criticism.* Philadelphia, 1940.

FELLOWES, E. H. *The English Madrigal Composers.* London, 1921.

PATTISON, BRUCE. *Music and Poetry of the English Renaissance.* London, 1948.

The Earlier Seventeenth Century (to 1660)

BIBLIOGRAPHY

"Literature of the Renaissance." Annually in *Studies in Philology,* 1917– .

RIBNER, IRVING. *Tudor and Stuart Drama.* New York, 1966.
  An excellent comprehensive guide.

LITERARY HISTORY

BENTLEY, GERALD EADES. *The Jacobean and Caroline Stage.* 7 vols. Oxford, 1941–1968.

BUSH, DOUGLAS. *English Literature in the Earlier Seventeenth Century, 1600–1660. (Oxford History of English Literature,* vol. V.) 2nd ed. Oxford, 1962.
  Excludes drama. Lucid, sensible, distinguished.

ELLIS-FERMOR, UNA. *Jacobean Drama.* 4th ed. London, 1958.

EMPSON, WILLIAM. *Seven Types of Ambiguity.* 3rd ed. London, 1953.
  A notable study.

GRIERSON, HERBERT J. C. *Cross Currents in English Literature of the Seventeenth Century.* London, 1929.

GRUNDY, JOAN. *The Spenserian Poets: A Study in Elizabethan and Jacobean Poetry.* London, 1969.
  Treats Michael Drayton, George Wither, William Browne, Giles and Phineas Fletcher.

KEAST, WILLIAM R., ed. *Seventeenth-Century English Poetry: Modern Essays in Criticism.* New York, 1962.

MARTZ, LOUIS L. *The Poetry of Meditation: A Study of English Religious Literature of the Seventeenth Century.* 2nd ed. New Haven, 1962.
  Crashaw, Donne, Milton, and others.

SUTHERLAND, JAMES. *English Literature in the Late Seventeenth Century. (Oxford History of English Literature,* vol. VI.) Oxford, 1969.
  Excellent.

SYPHER, WYLIE. *Four Stages of Renaissance Style.* New York, 1955.

TUVE, ROSEMOND. *Elizabethan and Metaphysical Imagery.* Chicago, 1947.

WEDGWOOD, C. V. *Seventeenth-Century English Literature.* London, 1950.
  Short and useful.

WILLIAMSON, GEORGE. *The Senecan Amble: A Study in Prose Style from Bacon to Collier.* Chicago, 1951.

POLITICAL, SOCIAL, AND INTELLECTUAL HISTORY

DAVIES, GODFREY. *The Early Stuarts, 1603–1660. (Oxford History of England,* vol. IX.) 2nd ed. Oxford, 1959.

LOVEJOY, A. C. *The Great Chain of Being.* Cambridge, Massachusetts, 1936.

   A seminal study in the history of ideas.

MAZZEO, JOSEPH ANTHONY. *Renaissance and Revolution: Backgrounds to Seventeenth-Century English Literature.* New York, 1965.

STONE, LAWRENCE. *The Crisis of the Aristocracy, 1558–1641.* Oxford, 1965.

TAWNEY, R. H. *Religion and the Rise of Capitalism.* New York, 1926.

   Of profound importance.

WILLEY, BASIL. *The Seventeenth-Century Background.* London, 1934.

   Intellectual history.

COLLECTIONS

AULT, NORMAN. *Seventeenth-Century Lyrics.* 2nd ed. London, 1950.

BALD, R. C. *Seventeenth-Century English Poetry.* New York, 1959.

BASKERVILL, C. R., et al. *Elizabethan and Stuart Plays.* New York, 1934.

   Contains forty-two plays.

GARDNER, HELEN. *The Metaphysical Poets.* London, 1957.

   A specially useful collection.

HARRIER, RICHARD C. *An Anthology of Jacobean Drama.* 2 vols. New York, 1963.

HEBEL, J. WILLIAM, and HOYT H. HUDSON. *Poetry of the English Renaissance, 1509–1660.* New York, 1929.

   A standard and generously representative anthology.

————. *Prose of the English Renaissance.* New York, 1952.

HENDERSON, PHILIP. *Shorter Novels: Jacobean and Restoration.* London, 1930.

   Ornatus and Artesia by Emmanuel Ford, *Oroonoko* by Aphra Behn, *The Isle of Pines* by Henry Neville, and *Incognita* by William Congreve.

MISH, CHARLES C. *The Anchor Anthology of Short Fiction of the Seventeenth Century*. Garden City, New York, 1963.
Contains ten tales.

WHITE, HELEN C., et al. *Seventeenth-Century Verse and Prose*. 2 vols. New York, 1952.
Well annotated.

WITHERSPOON, ALEXANDER M. and FRANK J. WARNKE. *Seventeenth-Century Prose and Poetry*. 2nd ed. New York, 1963.

THE ENGLISH BIBLE

Criticism

BRUCE, F. F. *The English Bible: A History of Translations*. New York, 1961.

BUTTERWORTH, CHARLES C. *The Literary Lineage of King James' Bible, 1340–1611*. Philadelphia, 1941.

DAICHES, DAVID. *The King James Version of the English Bible*. Chicago, 1941.

MOZLEY, J. F. *Coverdale and His Bibles*. London, 1953.

FRANCIS BACON (1561–1626)

Editions

JONES, R. F. *Essays, Advancement of Learning, New Atlantis, and Other Pieces*. New York, 1937.

SPEDDING, JAMES, et al. *Works*. 14 vols. London, 1857–1874.

Biography

STURT, MARY. *Francis Bacon*. London, 1932.

Criticism

ANDERSON, FULTON H. *Francis Bacon, His Career and His Thought*. Los Angeles, 1962.

JAMES, D. G. *The Dream of Learning*. Oxford, 1951.

WALLACE, KARL R. *Francis Bacon on Communication and Rhetoric*. Chapel Hill, North Carolina, 1943.

WILLIAMS, CHARLES. *Bacon*. London, 1933.

THOMAS MIDDLETON (ca. 1570–1627)

Edition

BULLEN, A. H. *Works*. 8 vols. London, 1885–1886.

Biography and Criticism

BARKER, RICHARD HINDREY. *Thomas Middleton*. New York, 1958.
DUNKEL, W. D. *The Dramatic Technique of Middleton in His Comedies*. Chicago, 1925.
SCHOENBAUM, SAMUEL. *Middleton's Tragedies*. New York, 1955.

JOHN DONNE (1572–1631)

Editions

GARDNER, HELEN. *The Divine Poems*. Oxford, 1952.
————. *The Elegies, and The Songs and Sonnets*. Oxford, 1965.
GRIERSON, HERBERT J. C. *Poems*. 2 vols. Oxford, 1912.
POTTER, GEORGE R., and EVELYN SIMPSON. *Sermons*. 10 vols. Berkeley, 1953–1962.
SHAWCROSS, JOHN. *Complete Poetry*. New York, 1967.

Biography

BALD, R. C. *John Donne*. Oxford, 1970.
 Definitive.
GOSSE, EDMUND. *Life and Letters*. 2 vols. London, 1899.

Criticism

GARDNER, HELEN, ed. *John Donne: A Collection of Critical Essays*. Englewood Cliffs, New Jersey, 1962.
LEISHMAN, J. B. *The Monarch of Wit*. 5th ed. London, 1962.
WEBBER, JOAN. *Contrary Music: The Prose Style of John Donne*. Madison, Wisconsin, 1963.

JOSEPH HALL (1574–1656)

Editions

DAVENPORT, ARNOLD. *Collected Poems*. Liverpool, 1949.
WYNTER, PHILIP. *Works*. 10 vols. Oxford, 1863.

CYRIL TOURNEUR (ca. 1575–1626)

Edition

NICOLL, ALLARDYCE. *Works.* London, 1930.

Criticism

MURRAY, PETER B. *A Study of Cyril Tourneur.* Philadelphia, 1964.

ROBERT BURTON (1577–1640)

Edition

DELL, FLOYD, and PAUL JORDAN-SMITH. *Anatomy of Melancholy.* 2 vols. New York, 1927.

Criticism

BABB, LAWRENCE. *Sanity in Bedlam.* East Lansing, Michigan, 1959.
MUELLER, WILLIAM R. *The Anatomy of Robert Burton's England.* Berkeley, 1952.

SIR THOMAS OVERBURY (1581–1613)

Edition

PAYLOR, W. J. *The Overburian Characters.* Oxford, 1936.

Biography and Criticism

MCELWEE, WILLIAM LLOYD. *The Murder of Sir Thomas Overbury.* London, 1952.

JOHN FORD (1586–ca. 1639)

Editions

BANG, W., and HENRY DE VOCHT. *Dramatic Works.* 2 vols. Louvain, 1908, 1927.
ELLIS, HAVELOCK. *Five Plays.* London, 1903.
    Reprinted in New York, 1957.

Criticism

LEECH, CLIFFORD. *John Ford and the Drama of His Time*. London, 1957.

STAVIG, MARK. *John Ford and the Traditional Moral Order*. Madison, Wisconsin, 1968.

THOMAS HOBBES (1588–1679)

Editions

MOLESWORTH, WILLIAM. *The English Works*. 11 vols. London, 1839–1845.

OAKESHOTT, MICHAEL. *Leviathan*. Oxford, 1946.

Criticism

MINTZ, SAMUEL I. *The Hunting of Leviathan*. Cambridge, 1962.

STRAUSS, LEO. *The Political Philosophy of Hobbes*. Chicago, 1952.

THORPE, C. D. *The Aesthetic Theory of Thomas Hobbes*. Ann Arbor, 1940.

WARRENDER, HOWARD. *The Political Philosophy of Hobbes*. Oxford, 1957.

ROBERT HERRICK (1591–1674)

Editions

HAYWARD, JOHN. *Selected Poems*. London, 1961.

MARTIN, L. C. *Poetical Works*. Oxford, 1956.

PATRICK, J. MAX. *Complete Poetry*. New York, 1963.

Biography and Criticism

CHUTE, MARCHETTE. *Two Gentle Men*. New York, 1959. Herrick and George Herbert.

HENRY KING (1592–1669)

Edition

CRUM, MARGARET. *Poems*. Oxford, 1965.

Criticism

BERMAN, RONALD. *Henry King and the Seventeenth Century.* London, 1964.

GEORGE HERBERT (1593–1633)

Edition

GARDNER, HELEN. *Poems.* 2nd ed. London, 1961.

Biography and Criticism

BOTTRALL, MARGARET. *George Herbert.* London, 1954.
CHUTE, MARCHETTE. *Two Gentle Men.* New York, 1959.
    Herbert and Herrick.
STEIN, ARNOLD. *George Herbert's Lyrics.* Baltimore, 1968.
SUMMERS, J. H. *George Herbert.* Cambridge, Massachusetts, 1954.
TUVE, ROSEMOND. *A Reading of George Herbert.* London, 1952.

IZAAK WALTON (1593–1683)

Edition

KEYNES, GEOFFREY. *The Compleat Walton.* London, 1929.

Criticism

COOPER, JOHN R. *The Art of the Compleat Angler.* Durham, North Carolina, 1968.
NOVARR, DAVID. *The Making of Walton's Lives.* Ithaca, New York, 1958.

SIR THOMAS CAREW (ca. 1594–1640)

Edition

DUNLAP, RHODES. *Poems.* Oxford, 1949.

Biography and Criticism

SELIG, E. I. *The Flourishing Wreath.* New Haven, 1958.

JAMES SHIRLEY (1596–1666)

Edition

GIFFORD, WILLIAM. *Dramatic Works and Poems.* 6 vols. London, 1833.
Reprinted in New York in 1966.

Biography and Criticism

FORSYTHE, ROBERT S. *The Relationship of Shirley's Plays to the Elizabethan Drama.* New York, 1914.
Reprinted, 1965.
NASON, ARTHUR H. *James Shirley, Dramatist.* New York, 1915.
Reprinted, 1967.

JOHN EARLE (ca. 1601–1665)

Edition

MURPHY, GWENDOLEN. *Micro-cosmographie.* London, 1928.

SIR THOMAS BROWNE (1605–1682)

Editions

ENDICOTT, NORMAN. *The Prose.* New York, 1967.
KEYNES, GEOFFREY. *Works.* New ed. 4 vols. London, 1964.
MARTIN, L. C. *Religio Medici and Other Works.* Oxford, 1964.

Biography and Criticism

BENNETT, JOAN. *Sir Thomas Browne.* Cambridge, 1962.
DUNN, WILLIAM P. *Sir Thomas Browne.* 2nd ed. Minneapolis, Minnesota, 1950.
FINCH, JEREMIAH S. *Sir Thomas Browne.* New York, 1950.
HUNTLEY, FRANK LIVINGSTONE. *Sir Thomas Browne.* Ann Arbor, 1962.

SIR WILLIAM DAVENANT (1606–1668)

Edition

MAIDMENT, JAMES, and W. H. LOGAN. *Dramatic Works.* 5 vols.
  Edinburgh, 1872–1874.
  Reissued in New York in 1964.

Biography and Criticism

COLLINS, HOWARD S. *The Comedy of Sir William Davenant.* The
  Hague, 1967.
HARBAGE, ALFRED. *Sir William Davenant: Poet-Venturer.* Philadel-
  phia, 1935.
NETHERCOT, ARTHUR H. *Sir William D'Avenant: Poet Laureate and
  Playwright-Manager.* Chicago, 1938.

EDMUND WALLER (1606–1687)

Edition

THORN-DRURY, G. *Poems.* 2 vols. London, 1905.

Criticism

ALLISON, ALEXANDER WARD. *Toward an Augustan Poetic.* Louisville, Kentucky, 1962.

THOMAS FULLER (1608–1661)

Edition

FREEMAN, JOHN. *The Worthies of England.* London, 1952.

Criticism

HOUGHTON, WALTER E. *The Formation of Thomas Fuller's Holy
  and Profane States.* Cambridge, Massachusetts, 1938.

JOHN MILTON (1608–1674)

Editions

HUGHES, MERRITT Y. *Complete Poems and Major Prose.* New York, 1957.
> The best one-volume edition.

PATTERSON, F. A., et al. *Works.* Columbia edition. 21 vols. New York, 1931–1940.

PRINCE, F. T. *Samson Agonistes.* London, 1957.
> The best edition, with excellent notes.

Guides

HANFORD, JAMES HOLLY. *Milton.* New York, 1966.
> An excellent bibliography.

——. *A Milton Handbook.* 5th ed. New York, 1969.
> An indispensable work.

NICOLSON, MARJORIE HOPE. *A Reader's Guide to Milton.* London, 1964.

Biography

HANFORD, JAMES HOLLY. *John Milton, Englishman.* New York, 1949.

PARKER, WILLIAM RILEY. *Milton: A Biography.* 2 vols. Oxford, 1968.

Criticism

BARKER, ARTHUR E., ed. *Milton: Modern Essays in Criticism.* New York, 1965.
> Essays by various critics.

BROADBENT, J. B. *Some Graver Subject: An Essay on "Paradise Lost."* New York, 1960.

BUSH, DOUGLAS. *John Milton.* New York, 1964.
> An excellent introduction to the man and his works.

EMPSON, WILLIAM. *Milton's God.* London, 1961.
> Controversial.

LEWIS, C. S. *A Preface to Paradise Lost.* Oxford, 1942.

MARTZ, LOUIS L., ed. *Milton: A Collection of Critical Essays.* Englewood Cliffs, New Jersey, 1966.
> Essays by various critics.

RICKS, CHRISTOPHER. *Milton's Grand Style.* Oxford, 1963.

TILLYARD, E. M. W. *Studies in Milton.* London, 1951.

WALDOCK, A. J. A. *Paradise Lost and Its Critics.* Cambridge, 1947.

EDWARD HYDE, EARL OF CLARENDON (1609–1674)

Edition

MACRAY, W. DUNN. *History of the Rebellion.* 6 vols. Oxford, 1888.

Biography

CRAIK, HENRY. *Life.* 2 vols. New York, 1911.

SIR JOHN SUCKLING (1609–1642)

Editions

BERRY, HERBERT. *Sir John Suckling's Poems and Letters from Manuscript.* London, Ontario, 1960.

THOMPSON, A. HAMILTON. *Works.* London, 1910.

RICHARD CRASHAW (ca. 1613–1649)

Edition

MARTIN, L. C. *Poems.* 2nd ed. Oxford, 1957.

Biography and Criticism

WALLERSTEIN, RUTH C. *Richard Crashaw.* Madison, Wisconsin, 1935.

WARREN, AUSTIN. *Richard Crashaw.* University, Louisiana, 1939.
> The best modern study.

ABRAHAM COWLEY (1618–1667)

Editions

MARTIN, L. C. *Poetry and Prose.* Oxford, 1949.

WALLER, A. R. *English Writings.* 2 vols. Cambridge, 1905–1906.

Biography

NETHERCOT, ARTHUR H. *Abraham Cowley: The Muse's Hannibal.* Oxford, 1931.

Criticism

HINMAN, ROBERT B. *Abraham Cowley's World of Order.* Cambridge, Massachusetts, 1960.

RICHARD LOVELACE (1618–1657)

Edition

WILKINSON, C. H. *Poems.* 2nd ed. Oxford, 1930.

ANDREW MARVELL (1621–1678)

Editions

LORD, GEORGE DE FOREST. *Complete Poetry.* New Haven, 1968.

MARGOLIOUTH, H. M. *Poems and Letters.* 2nd ed. 2 vols. Oxford, 1952.

Criticism

BRADBROOK, M. C., and M. G. LLOYD THOMAS. *Andrew Marvell.* 2nd ed. Cambridge, 1961.

LEISHMAN, J. B. *The Art of Marvell's Poetry.* London, 1966.

LORD, GEORGE DE FOREST, ed. *Andrew Marvell: A Collection of Critical Essays.* Englewood Cliffs, New Jersey, 1968.
Essays by various critics.

TOLIVER, HAROLD E. *Marvell's Ironic Vision.* New Haven, 1965.

WALLACE, JOHN. *Destiny His Choice: The Loyalism of Andrew Marvell.* Cambridge, 1968.

HENRY VAUGHAN (1621–1695)

Editions

FOGLE, FRENCH. *Complete Poetry.* Garden City, New York, 1964.
MARTIN, L. C. *Poetry and Selected Prose.* London, 1963.
————. *Works.* 2nd ed. Oxford, 1957.

Biography

HUTCHINSON, F. E. *Henry Vaughan.* Oxford, 1947.
Standard.

Criticism

DURR, R. A. *On the Mystical Poetry of Henry Vaughan.* Cambridge,
Massachusetts, 1962.
GARNER, ROSS. *Henry Vaughan.* Chicago, 1959.
PETTET, E. C. *Of Paradise and Light.* Cambridge, 1960.

JOHN BUNYAN (1628–1688)

Editions

STEBBING, HENRY. *Works.* 4 vols. London, 1859–1860.
WHARREY, J. B. *The Pilgrim's Progress.* Revised ed. by Roger Shar-
rock. London, 1960.
Fully annotated.

Biography

BROWN, JOHN. *John Bunyan.* Revised ed. by F. M. Harrison. Lon-
don, 1928.
The standard biography.
HARRISON, G. B. *John Bunyan.* London, 1928.
TALON, HENRI. *John Bunyan.* Trans. Barbara Wall. London, 1951.
A life-and-works study translated from the French.

Criticism

SHARROCK, ROGER. *John Bunyan.* London, 1954.
TINDALL, WILLIAM YORK. *John Bunyan, Mechanick Preacher.* New
York, 1934.

THOMAS TRAHERNE (1637–1674)

Edition

MARGOLIOUTH, H. M. *Centuries, Poems, and Thanksgivings.* 2 vols. Oxford, 1958.

Biography and Criticism

WADE, GLADYS I. *Thomas Traherne.* 2nd ed. Princeton, 1946.

The Restoration and the Eighteenth Century (1660–1800)

BIBLIOGRAPHY

"English Literature, 1660–1800: A Current Bibliography [1925–]." Annually in *Philological Quarterly,* 1926– .

The issues for 1925–1960 are collected (and indexed) in Louis A. Landa, et al., *English Literature, 1660–1800: A Bibliography of Modern Studies* (4 vols., Princeton, 1950–1952, 1962).

LITERARY HISTORY

CLIFFORD, JAMES L., ed. *Eighteenth-Century English Literature: Modern Essays in Criticism.* New York, 1959.

Essays by various scholars.

DOBRÉE, BONAMY. *English Literature in the Earlier Eighteenth Century.* (*Oxford History of English Literature,* vol. VII.) Oxford, 1959.

Thorough.

ELTON, OLIVER. *A Survey of English Literature, 1730–1780.* 2 vols. London, 1928.

Old-fashioned, but elegantly written.

LOFTIS, JOHN. *Restoration Drama: Modern Essays in Criticism.* New York, 1966.

Essays by various scholars.

MCKILLOP, ALAN DUGALD. *English Literature from Dryden to Burns.* New York, 1948.

Sound and economical.

MINER, EARL, ed. *Restoration Dramatists.* Englewood Cliffs, New Jersey, 1966.

Essays by various scholars.

SHERBURN, GEORGE. *The Restoration and Eighteenth Century (1660–1789).* (Albert C. Baugh, et al., *A Literary History of England,* vol. III.) 2nd ed., revised by Donald F. Bond. New York, 1967.

The best of the surveys, available separately.

STEPHEN, LESLIE. *English Literature and Society in the Eighteenth Century.* London, 1904.

Despite its date, a fine introduction.

SUTHERLAND, JAMES. *English Literature in the Late Seventeenth Century.* (*Oxford History of English Literature,* vol. VI.) Oxford, 1969.

Excellent.

————. *A Preface to Eighteenth-Century Poetry*. Oxford, 1948.
An excellent introduction to the subject.

WILSON, JOHN HAROLD. *A Preface to Restoration Drama*. Boston, 1965.
Crisp and authoritative.

POLITICAL, SOCIAL, AND INTELLECTUAL HISTORY

BECKER, CARL L. *The Heavenly City of the Eighteenth-Century Philosophers*. New Haven, 1932.
An extremely influential book, no longer accepted without reservation.

CLARK, G. N. *The Later Stuarts, 1660–1714*. (*Oxford History of England*, vol. X.) 2nd ed. Oxford, 1956.

GREENE, DONALD. *The Age of Exuberance: Backgrounds to Eighteenth-Century English Literature*. New York, 1970.

HUMPHREYS, A. R. *The Augustan World*. London, 1954.
A very good introduction to the period.

JOHNSON, JAMES WILLIAM. *The Formation of English Neo Classical Thought*. Princeton, 1967.

LOVEJOY, ARTHUR O. *The Great Chain of Being*. Cambridge, Massachusetts, 1936.
An important study in the history of ideas.

PLUMB, J. H. *England in the Eighteenth Century*. London, 1950.
Excellent.

WATSON, J. STEVEN. *The Reign of George III, 1760–1815*. (*Oxford History of England*, vol. XII.) Oxford, 1960.

WILLEY, BASIL. *The Eighteenth-Century Background*. London, 1940.
Intellectual history.

————. *The Seventeenth-Century Background*. London, 1934.
Intellectual history.

WILLIAMS, BASIL. *The Whig Supremacy, 1714–1760*. (*Oxford History of England*, vol. XI.) 2nd ed., revised by C. H. Stuart. Oxford, 1962.
Controversial.

COLLECTIONS

BRADY, FRANK, and MARTIN PRICE. *English Prose and Poetry, 1660–1800*. New York, 1961.
A convenient collection that excludes Dryden, Pope, Swift, Johnson, and Blake (as well as the novelists).

BREDVOLD, LOUIS I., et al. *Eighteenth-Century Poetry and Prose.* 2nd ed. New York, 1956.

Enormous but generously inclusive and well annotated. Now superseded by the Tillotson-Fussell-Waingrow collection.

KINSLEY, JAMES. *The Oxford Book of Ballads.* New York, 1970.

LORD, GEORGE DE FOREST, et al. *Poems on Affairs of State: Augustan Satirical Verse, 1660–1714.* New Haven, 1963–   .
In progress.

NETTLETON, GEORGE H., and ARTHUR E. CASE. *British Dramatists from Dryden to Sheridan.* Boston, 1939.

Twenty-five plays.

PAGLIARO, HAROLD E. *Major English Writers of the Eighteenth Century.* New York, 1969.

A beautifully produced collection, to be followed by another containing critical prose.

PETTIT, HENRY. *A Collection of English Prose, 1660–1800.* New York, 1962.

QUINTANA, RICARDO, and ALVIN WHITLEY. *English Poetry of the Mid and Late Eighteenth Century.* New York, 1963.

SPACKS, PATRICIA MEYER. *Eighteenth-Century Poetry.* Englewood Cliffs, New Jersey, 1964.

SUTHERLAND, JAMES. *Early Eighteenth-Century Poetry.* London, 1965.

SWEDENBERG, H. T., JR. *English Poetry of the Restoration and Early Eighteenth Century.* New York, 1968.

TILLOTSON, GEOFFREY, et al. *Eighteenth-Century English Literature.* New York, 1969.

Comprehensive, scholarly, readable. This will no doubt be the standard collection for many years to come.

WILSON, JOHN HAROLD. *Six Eighteenth-Century Plays.* Boston, 1963.
From Rowe's *The Fair Penitent* (1703) through Sheridan's *The School for Scandal* (1777).

SAMUEL BUTLER (1612–1680)

Editions

LAMAR, RENE. *Satires and Miscellaneous Poetry and Prose.* Cambridge, 1928.

WILDERS, JOHN. *Hudibras.* New York, 1968.
The definitive edition, with full commentary.

Criticism

RICHARDS, EDWARD A. *Hudibras in the Burlesque Tradition.* New York, 1937.

JOHN EVELYN (1620–1706)

Edition

DEBEER, E. S. *Diary.* 6 vols. Oxford, 1955.
A one-volume edition, without the notes, was issued in 1959.

Biography

HISCOCK, W. G. *John Evelyn and Mrs. Godolphin.* London, 1951. Continued in *John Evelyn and His Family Circle,* London, 1955.

JOHN AUBREY (1626–1697)

Edition

DICK, OLIVER LAWSON. *Brief Lives.* 3rd ed. London, 1960.
Selections.

Biography

POWELL, ANTHONY. *John Aubrey and His Friends.* Revised ed. New York, 1963.

JOHN DRYDEN (1631–1700)

Editions

HOOKER, E. N., et al. *Works.* Berkeley, 1956–
The definitive edition—the California Dryden—in progress.
KINSLEY, JAMES. *Poems and Fables.* Oxford, 1962.
MINER, EARL. *Selected Poetry and Prose.* New York, 1969.
SCOTT, WALTER. *Works.* 18 vols. London, 1808.
A revised edition was issued 1882–1893 under the editorship of George Saintsbury.
WATSON, GEORGE. *Of Dramatic Poesy and Other Critical Essays.* 2 vols. London, 1962–1964.

Biography

WARD, CHARLES E. *The Life of John Dryden.* Chapel Hill, North Carolina, 1961.
Now the standard biography.

Criticism

BREDVOLD, LOUIS I. *The Intellectual Milieu of John Dryden.* Ann
Arbor, 1934.
Indispensable.

MINER, EARL. *Dryden's Poetry.* Bloomington, Indiana, 1967.
A superb though selective study.

RAMSEY, PAUL. *The Art of John Dryden.* Louisville, Kentucky, 1968.

SCHILLING, BERNARD N., ed. *Dryden: A Collection of Critical Essays.* Englewood Cliffs, New Jersey, 1963.
Essays by various critics.

SWEDENBERG, H. T., JR., ed. *Essential Articles for the Study of John Dryden.* Hamden, Connecticut, 1966.
A wide-ranging selection.

VAN DOREN, MARK. *John Dryden: A Study of His Poetry.* 2nd ed.
London, 1946.
A useful guide.

SAMUEL PEPYS (1633–1703)

Editions

HEATH, HELEN TRUESDELL. *Letters.* Oxford, 1955.
WHEATLEY, HENRY B. *Diary.* 10 vols. London, 1893–1899.
The standard edition.

Biography and Criticism

BRYANT, ARTHUR. *Samuel Pepys.* 3 vols. Cambridge, 1933–1938.
A masterful biography which is also a portrait of the age.

NICOLSON, MARJORIE HOPE. *Pepys' Diary and the New Science.*
Charlottesville, Virginia, 1965.

SIR GEORGE ETHEREGE (1635–1691)

Editions

BRETT-SMITH, H. F. B. *Dramatic Works.* 2 vols. Oxford, 1927.
THORPE, JAMES. *Poems.* Princeton, 1963.

Biography and Criticism

UNDERWOOD, DALE. *Etherege and the Seventeenth Century Comedy
of Manners.* New Haven, 1957.

WILLIAM WYCHERLEY (1640–1716)

Edition

WEALES, GERALD. *Complete Plays.* New York, 1966.

Biography and Criticism

CONNELY, WILLARD. *Brawny Wycherley.* New York, 1930.
HOLLAND, NORMAN. *The First Modern Comedies.* Cambridge, Massachusetts, 1959.
　On Etherege, Wycherley, Congreve.
ZIMBARDO, ROSE A. *Wycherley's Drama.* New Haven, 1965.

JOHN WILMOT, EARL OF ROCHESTER (1647–1680)

Editions

DE SOLA PINTO, V. *Poems.* 2nd ed. Cambridge, Massachusetts, 1964.
HAYWARD, JOHN. *Collected Works.* London, 1926.
VIETH, DAVID M. *Complete Poems.* New Haven, 1968.

Biography and Criticism

DE SOLA PINTO, V. *Enthusiast in Wit.* Revised ed. London, 1962.

THOMAS OTWAY (1652–1685)

Edition

GHOSH, J. G. *Works.* 2 vols. Oxford, 1932.

Biography and Criticism

HAM, ROSWELL G. *Otway and Lee.* London, 1931.

DANIEL DEFOE (ca. 1660–1731)

Editions

————. *Novels and Selected Writings.* 14 vols. Oxford, 1927–1928.
HEALEY, GEORGE HARRIS. *Letters.* Oxford, 1955.

Biography and Criticism

MOORE, JOHN ROBERT. *Daniel Defoe: Citizen of the Modern World.* Chicago, 1958.

NOVAK, MAXIMILIAN E. *Defoe and the Nature of Man.* London, 1963.

————. *Economics and the Fiction of Daniel Defoe.* Berkeley, 1962.

SHINAGEL, MICHAEL. *Daniel Defoe and Middle-Class Gentility.* Cambridge, Massachusetts, 1968.

STARR, G. A. *Defoe and Spiritual Autobiography.* Princeton, 1965.

SUTHERLAND, JAMES R. *Defoe.* 2nd ed. London, 1950.
Definitive.

MATTHEW PRIOR (1664–1721)

Edition

WRIGHT, H. BUNKER, and MONROE K. SPEARS. *Literary Works.* 2 vols. Oxford, 1959.

Biography and Criticism

EVES, CHARLES K. *Matthew Prior: Poet and Diplomatist.* New York, 1939.

SIR JOHN VANBRUGH (1664–1726)

Editions

DOBRÉE, BONAMY, and GEOFFREY WEBB. *Complete Works.* 4 vols. London, 1927–1928.

SWAIN, A. E. H. *Sir John Vanbrugh.* London, 1896.
Revised in 1949.

Biography and Criticism

WHISTLER, LAURENCE. *Sir John Vanbrugh.* London, 1938.

JONATHAN SWIFT (1667–1745)

Editions

DAVIS, HERBERT. *Prose Works.* 15 vols. Oxford, 1939–1964.
Omits the *Journal to Stella.*

WILLIAMS, HAROLD. *Correspondence.* 5 vols. Oxford, 1963–1965.

WILLIAMS, HAROLD. *Journal to Stella.* 2 vols. Oxford, 1948.
———. *Poems.* 2nd ed. 3 vols. Oxford, 1958.

Biography

CRAIK, HENRY. *The Life of Jonathan Swift.* 2nd ed. 2 vols. London, 1894.
  Not yet entirely superseded.
EHRENPREIS, IRVIN. *Swift: The Man, His Works, and the Age.* 2 vols. Cambridge, Massachusetts, 1962, 1968.
  The definitive life, to be completed in three volumes.
VAN DOREN, CARL. *Swift.* New York, 1930.
  Readable.

Criticism

CASE, ARTHUR E. *Four Essays on Gulliver's Travels.* Princeton, 1945.
DAVIS, HERBERT. *Jonathan Swift.* Oxford, 1964.
  A series of essays.
DONOGHUE, DENIS. *Jonathan Swift: A Critical Introduction.* Cambridge, 1969.
JOHNSON, MAURICE. *The Sin of Wit: Jonathan Swift as a Poet.* Syracuse, New York, 1950.
PRICE, MARTIN. *Swift's Rhetorical Art.* New Haven, 1953.
QUINTANA, RICARDO. *The Mind and Art of Jonathan Swift.* 2nd ed. New York, 1953.
———. *Swift: An Introduction.* London, 1955.
  An excellent introduction.
TRAUGOTT, JOHN, ed. *Discussions of Swift.* Boston, 1962.
  Essays by various critics.
TUVESON, ERNEST, ed. *Swift: A Collection of Critical Essays.* Englewood Cliffs, New Jersey, 1964.
  Essays by various critics.
WILLIAMS, KATHLEEN. *Jonathan Swift and the Age of Compromise.* Lawrence, Kansas, 1958.

WILLIAM CONGREVE (1670–1731)

Editions

DAVIS, HERBERT. *Complete Plays.* Chicago, 1967.
DOBRÉE, BONAMY. *Works.* 2 vols. Oxford, 1925–1928.
SUMMERS, MONTAGUE. *Complete Works.* 4 vols. London, 1923.

Biography

HODGES, JOHN C. *William Congreve, the Man.* New York, 1941.

Criticism

FUJIMURA, THOMAS E. *The Restoration Comedy of Wit.* Princeton, 1952.

MUESCHKE, PAUL, and MIRIAM MUESCHKE. *A New View of Congreve's Way of the World.* Ann Arbor, 1958.

TAYLOR, D. CRANE. *William Congreve.* Oxford, 1931.

JOSEPH ADDISON (1672–1719) and RICHARD STEELE (1672–1729)

Editions

ALLEN, ROBERT J. *The Tatler and The Spectator.* New York, 1957. Selections.

BLANCHARD, RAE. *Correspondence of Richard Steele.* London, 1941.

BOND, DONALD F. *The Spectator.* 5 vols. Oxford, 1964.

GIBBS, LEWIS. *The Tatler.* New York, 1953.

GRAHAM, WALTER. *Letters of Joseph Addison.* Oxford, 1941.

Biography

AITKEN, GEORGE A. *Richard Steele.* 2 vols. London, 1889.

CONNELY, WILLARD. *Sir Richard Steele.* New York, 1934.

SMITHERS, PETER. *The Life of Joseph Addison.* Oxford, 1954.

WINTON, CALHOUN. *Captain Steele.* Baltimore, 1964.

Criticism

GRAHAM, WALTER. *English Literary Periodicals.* New York, 1930.

LOFTIS, JOHN. *Steele at Drury Lane.* Berkeley, 1952.

GEORGE FARQUHAR (1678–1707)

Editions

ARCHER, WILLIAM. *George Farquhar.* London, 1906. Reissued in 1959.

STONEHILL, CHARLES. *Complete Works.* 2 vols. London, 1930.

Biography and Criticism

ROTHSTEIN, ERIC. *George Farquhar.* New York, 1967.

JOHN GAY (1685–1732)

Editions

BURGESS, C. F. *Letters.* Oxford, 1966.
FABER, G. C. *Poetical Works.* Oxford, 1926.

Biography and Criticism

ARMENS, SVEN M. *John Gay, Social Critic.* New York, 1954.
GAGEY, E. M. *The Ballad Opera.* New York, 1937.
IRVING, W. H. *John Gay: Favorite of the Wits.* Durham, North Carolina, 1940.
SPACKS, PATRICIA MEYER. *John Gay.* New York, 1965.

ALEXANDER POPE (1688–1744)

Editions

AULT, NORMAN. *Prose Works.* Vol. I, 1711–1720. Oxford, 1935. Never completed.
BUTT, JOHN, et al. *Poems.* Twickenham edition. 6 vols. London, 1939–1962.
A one-volume edition, shorn of much of the apparatus, was issued in 1963.
SHERBURN, GEORGE. *Correspondence.* 5 vols. Oxford, 1956.
WILLIAMS, AUBREY. *Poetry and Prose.* Boston, 1969.
The best one-volume selection.
WIMSATT, W. K. *Selected Poetry and Prose.* New York, 1951.
A convenient selection.

Biography

AULT, NORMAN. *New Light on Pope.* London, 1949.
SHERBURN, GEORGE. *The Early Career of Alexander Pope.* Oxford, 1934.
To 1727 only.

Criticism

BLANSHARD, RUFUS A., ed. *Discussions of Alexander Pope.* Boston, 1960.
Essays by various critics.

BROWER, REUBEN A. *Alexander Pope: The Poetry of Allusion.* Oxford, 1959.
The best single introduction to Pope's poetry.

MACK, MAYNARD, ed. *Essential Articles for the Study of Alexander Pope.* Hamden, Connecticut, 1964.
Essays by various critics.

ROOT, R. K. *The Poetical Career of Alexander Pope.* Princeton, 1938.
Sound.

TILLOTSON, GEOFFREY. *On the Poetry of Pope.* 2nd ed. Oxford, 1950.

———. *Pope and Human Nature.* Oxford, 1958.

WILLIAMS, AUBREY L. *Pope's 'Dunciad.'* Baton Rouge, Louisiana, 1955.
An excellent study.

SAMUEL RICHARDSON (1689–1761)

Editions

———. *The Novels.* 18 vols. Oxford, 1929–1931.
Richardson's novels are notoriously long, but there is a useful abridgment of *Clarissa,* edited by George Sherburn, Boston, 1962.

CARROLL, JOHN. *Selected Letters.* Oxford, 1964.

Biography and Criticism

CARROLL, JOHN, ed. *Samuel Richardson: A Collection of Critical Essays.* Englewood Cliffs, New Jersey, 1969.
Essays by various critics.

GOLDEN, MORRIS. *Richardson's Characters.* Ann Arbor, 1963.

KONIGSBERG, IRA. *Samuel Richardson and the Dramatic Novel.* Louisville, Kentucky, 1968.

McKILLOP, ALAN DUGALD. *Samuel Richardson, Printer and Novelist.* Chapel Hill, North Carolina, 1936.
Standard.

SALE, WILLIAM M., JR. *Samuel Richardson, Master Printer.* Ithaca, New York, 1950.

PHILIP DORMER STANHOPE, LORD CHESTERFIELD (1694–1773)

Editions

DOBRÉE, BONAMY. *Letters.* 6 vols. London, 1932.
GULICK, SIDNEY L. *Unpublished Letters.* Berkeley, 1937.
Pendant to Dobrée.

Biography and Criticism

SHELLABARGER, SAMUEL. *Lord Chesterfield and His World.* Boston, 1951.

JAMES THOMSON (1700–1748)

Editions

McKILLOP, ALAN DUGALD. *The Castle of Indolence and Other Poems.* Lawrence, Kansas, 1961.
———. *James Thomson: Letters and Documents.* Lawrence, Kansas, 1958.
ROBERTSON, J. LOGIE. *Complete Poetical Works.* Oxford, 1908.

Biography and Criticism

COHEN, RALPH. *The Art of Discrimination.* Berkeley, 1964.
GRANT, DOUGLAS. *James Thomson.* London, 1951.
A study of the life and works.
McKILLOP, ALAN DUGALD. *The Background of Thomson's Seasons.* Minneapolis, Minnesota, 1942.

HENRY FIELDING (1707–1754)

Editions

COLEY, WILLIAM B., et al. *The Wesleyan Edition of the Works.* Middletown, Connecticut, 1967–   .
The definitive edition, in progress.
HENLEY, WILLIAM ERNEST. *Complete Works.* 16 vols. New York, 1902.

Biography and Criticism

BATTESTIN, MARTIN. *The Moral Basis of Fielding's Art.* Middletown, Connecticut, 1959.

BUTT, JOHN. *Fielding.* Revised ed. London, 1959.
Brief, pointed, valuable.

CROSS, WILBUR L. *The History of Henry Fielding.* 3 vols. New Haven, 1918.
Standard though old-fashioned and too lengthy.

HATFIELD, GLENN W. *Henry Fielding and the Language of Irony.* Chicago, 1968.

PAULSON, RONALD, ed. *Fielding: A Collection of Critical Essays.* Englewood Cliffs, New Jersey, 1962.
Essays by various critics.

WRIGHT, ANDREW. *Henry Fielding: Mask and Feast.* London, 1965.

SAMUEL JOHNSON (1709–1784)

Editions

BATE, WALTER JACKSON. *Selected Essays from the Rambler, Adventurer, and Idler.* New Haven, 1968.

CHAPMAN, R. W. *Letters.* 3 vols. Oxford, 1952.

———. *Selections.* 2nd ed. Oxford, 1962.
Useful.

CRUTTWELL, PATRICK. *Selected Writings.* Baltimore, 1968.

HAZEN, ALLEN T., et al. *Works.* New Haven, 1958–   .
The definitive edition, in progress.

HILL, GEORGE BIRKBECK. *Lives of the English Poets.* 3 vols. Oxford, 1905.
Still the most useful criticism of a number of seventeenth- and eighteenth-century poets especially.

KEAST, W. R. *Critical Essays.* New York, 1955.
Excludes the *Lives of the Poets.*

Biography

BOSWELL, JAMES. *The Life of Samuel Johnson* (1791), ed. George Birkbeck Hill and L. F. Powell. 6 vols. Oxford, 1934–1950.
The definitive edition; but a one-volume edition, edited by R. W. Chapman, was issued in 1953. This is the best one-volume edition, and it has an excellent index.

CLIFFORD, JAMES L. *Young Sam Johnson.* New York, 1955.
Good on the early years, scamped by Boswell.

GREENE, DONALD J. *The Politics of Samuel Johnson.* New Haven, 1960.

KRUTCH, JOSEPH WOOD. *Samuel Johnson.* New York, 1944.
Readable.

Criticism

BATE, WALTER JACKSON. *The Achievement of Samuel Johnson.* New York, 1955.

BRONSON, B. H. *Johnson Agonistes.* Cambridge, 1946.

GREENE, DONALD J., ed. *Samuel Johnson: A Collection of Critical Essays.* Englewood Cliffs, New Jersey, 1965.
Essays by various critics.

HAGSTRUM, JEAN H. *Samuel Johnson's Literary Criticism.* Revised ed. Chicago, 1967.

SHERBO, ARTHUR. *Samuel Johnson, Editor of Shakespeare.* Urbana, Illinois, 1956.

WIMSATT, WILLIAM K. *The Prose Style of Samuel Johnson.* New Haven, 1941.
Important.

LAURENCE STERNE (1713–1768)

Editions

CROSS, WILBUR L. *Works.* 12 vols. New York, 1904.

CURTIS, L. P. *Letters.* Oxford, 1935.

JACK, IAN. *A Sentimental Journey.* London, 1968.
Includes the *Journal to Eliza* and *A Political Romance,* Sterne's almost unknown early satire.

STOUT, GARDNER D., JR. *A Sentimental Journey.* Berkeley, 1967.
Authoritative.

WATT, IAN. *Tristram Shandy.* Boston, 1965.
Impeccably edited, well annotated.

WORK, JAMES A. *Tristram Shandy.* New York, 1940.
Contains the fullest annotations.

Biography and Criticism

CROSS, WILBUR L. *The Life and Times of Laurence Sterne.* 2 vols. 3rd ed. New Haven, 1929.

CURTIS, L. P. *The Politicks of Laurence Sterne.* London, 1929.

FLUCHÈRE, HENRI. *Laurence Sterne.* Trans. Barbara Bray. Oxford, 1965.

TRAUGOTT, JOHN. *Tristram Shandy's World.* Berkeley, 1955.

THOMAS GRAY (1716–1771)

Editions

CRAFTS, J. *Poetry and Prose*. Oxford, 1926.
A selection.

STARR, H. N., and J. R. HENDRICKSON. *Complete Poems*. Oxford, 1966.
The definitive edition.

TOYNBEE, PAGET, and LEONARD WHIBLEY. *Correspondence*. 3 vols. Oxford, 1935.

Biography

JONES, W. POWELL. *Thomas Gray, Scholar*. Cambridge, Massachusetts, 1937.

KETTON-CREMER, R. W. *Thomas Gray: A Biography*. Cambridge, 1955.

Criticism

GOLDEN, MORRIS. *Thomas Gray*. New York, 1964.

REED, AMY LOUISE. *The Background of Gray's Elegy*. New York, 1924.

HORACE WALPOLE (1717–1797)

Editions

BERRY, MARY, et al. *Works*. 9 vols. 1798–1825.

LEWIS, W. S. *Correspondence*. New Haven, 1937– .
In progress.

Biography and Criticism

KETTON-CREMER, R. W. *Horace Walpole*. Revised ed. London, 1946.

WILLIAM COLLINS (1721–1759)

Edition

STONE, CHRISTOPHER, and AUSTIN LANE POOLE. *The Poems of Gray and Collins*. London, 1936.

Biography and Criticism

AINSWORTH, EDWARD GAY, JR. *Poor Collins*. Ithaca, New York, 1937.
Life and works.
GARROD, H. W. *Collins*. Oxford, 1928.
SIGWORTH, OLIVER F. *William Collins*. New York, 1965.

TOBIAS GEORGE SMOLLETT (1721–1771)

Editions

————. *Novels*. 11 vols. Oxford, 1925–1926.
NOYES, EDWARD S. *Letters*. Cambridge, Massachusetts, 1926.

Biography

KNAPP, LEWIS M. *Tobias Smollett*. Princeton, 1949.
MARTZ, LOUIS L. *The Later Career of Tobias Smollett*. New Haven, 1942.

Criticism

GOLDBERG, M. A. *Smollett and the Scottish School*. Albuquerque, New Mexico, 1959.
SPECTOR, ROBERT DONALD. *Tobias Smollett*. New York, 1968.

CHRISTOPHER SMART (1722–1771)

Editions

BOND, W. H. *Jubilate Agno*. Cambridge, Massachusetts, 1954.
CALLAN, NORMAN. *Collected Poems*. 2 vols. London, 1949.

Biography and Criticism

BLAYDES, SOPHIA B. *Christopher Smart*. The Hague, 1966.
DEVLIN, CHRISTOPHER. *Poor Kit Smart*. Carbondale, Illinois, 1961.
SHERBO, ARTHUR. *Christopher Smart: Scholar of the University*. East Lansing, Michigan, 1967.

EDMUND BURKE (1729–1797)

Editions

BATE, WALTER JACKSON. *Selected Works*. New York, 1960.
COPELAND, THOMAS W. *Correspondence*. Cambridge, 1958–   .
The definitive edition, in progress.

Biography and Criticism

COPELAND, THOMAS W. *Our Eminent Friend Edmund Burke.* New Haven, 1949.
MAGNUS, PHILIP. *Edmund Burke: A Life.* London, 1939.

OLIVER GOLDSMITH (ca. 1730–1774)

Editions

BALDERSTON, KATHARINE C. *Collected Letters.* Cambridge, 1928.
FRIEDMAN, ARTHUR. *Works.* 5 vols. Chicago, 1965.
Definitive.

Biography and Criticism

WARDLE, RALPH M. *Oliver Goldsmith.* Lawrence, Kansas, 1957.

WILLIAM COWPER (1731–1800)

Editions

JEFFARES, A. NORMAN. *Selected Poems and Letters.* London, 1963.
Contains a useful introduction.
SPILLER, BRIAN. *Poetry and Prose.* London, 1969.
A well-regarded selection.
VAN DOREN, MARK. *Selected Letters.* New York, 1951.

Biography and Criticism

CECIL, LORD DAVID. *The Stricken Deer.* London, 1929.
GOLDEN, MORRIS. *In Search of Stability.* New York, 1960.
HARTLEY, LODWICK. *William Cowper: The Continuing Revaluation.* Chapel Hill, North Carolina, 1960.
A survey and bibliography.
QUINLAN, MAURICE J. *William Cowper.* Minneapolis, Minnesota, 1953.
RYSKAMP, CHARLES. *William Cowper of the Inner Temple.* Cambridge, 1959.
THOMAS, GILBERT. *William Cowper and the Eighteenth Century.* 2nd ed. London, 1948.

EDWARD GIBBON (1737–1794)

Editions

BURY, J. B. *The History of the Decline and Fall of the Roman Empire.* 7 vols. London, 1896–1900.
A revised edition was published in 1926–1929. An excellent one-volume abridgment was issued in 1960.

NORTON, J. E. *Letters.* 3 vols. London, 1956.

SAUNDERS, DERO A. *Autobiography.* New York, 1961.
Restores suppressed passages.

Biography and Criticism

BOND, HAROLD L. *The Literary Art of Edward Gibbon.* Oxford, 1960.

LOW, D. M. *Edward Gibbon.* London, 1937.

WEDGWOOD, C. V. *Edward Gibbon.* London, 1954.

YOUNG, G. M. *Gibbon.* 2nd ed. London, 1948.

JAMES BOSWELL (1740–1795)

Editions

HILL, GEORGE BIRKBECK, and L. F. POWELL. *The Life of Samuel Johnson.* 6 vols. Oxford, 1934–1950.
The definitive edition; but a one-volume edition, edited by R. W. Chapman, was issued in 1953. This is the best one-volume edition, and it has an excellent index.

POTTLE, FREDERICK A. *Journals.* New Haven, 1950– .
In progress. The *London Journal* is more interesting than the others.

POTTLE, FREDERICK A., and CHARLES H. BENNET. *A Journal of a Tour to the Hebrides.* New York, 1936.

SCOTT, GEOFFREY, and FREDERICK A. POTTLE. *The Private Papers.* 18 vols. Mount Vernon, New York, 1928–1934.

TINKER, CHAUNCEY B. *Letters.* 2 vols. Oxford, 1924.

Biography

POTTLE, FREDERICK A. *James Boswell: The Early Years.* New Haven, 1966.

The definitive biography, superseding earlier biographies because based on the Boswell papers that have come to light in the last four decades.

SMITH-DAMPIER, JOHN L. *Who's Who in Boswell.* Oxford, 1935.

RICHARD BRINSLEY SHERIDAN (1751-1816)

Editions

PRICE, C. J. L. *Letters.* 3 vols. New York, 1966.
RHODES, R. CROMPTON. *Plays and Poems.* 3 vols. Oxford, 1928.

Biography and Criticism

DARLINGTON, W. A. *Sheridan.* London, 1951.
RHODES, R. CROMPTON. *Harlequin Sheridan.* Oxford, 1933.

FANNY BURNEY (1752-1840)

Editions

MACKINNON, FRANK. *Evelina.* Oxford, 1930.
MASEFIELD, MURIEL. *Diary and Letters.* London, 1931.

Biography

HEMLOW, JOYCE. *The History of Fanny Burney.* Oxford, 1958.

Criticism

WHITE, EUGENE. *Fanny Burney, Novelist.* Hamden, Connecticut, 1960.

GEORGE CRABBE (1754-1832)

Edition

WARD, A. W. *Works.* 3 vols. Cambridge, 1905.

Biography and Criticism

CHAMBERLAIN, ROBERT L. *George Crabbe.* New York, 1965.
HADDAKIN, LILLIAN. *The Poetry of Crabbe.* London, 1955.

WILLIAM BLAKE (1757–1827)

Editions

BATESON, F. W. *Selected Poems.* London, 1957.
A good selection, with very helpful notes.
ERDMAN, DAVID V. *The Poetry and Prose of William Blake.* New York, 1964.
Authoritative, but too austerely unpunctuated for general use.
KEYNES, GEOFFREY. *Poetry and Prose.* New ed. London, 1966.
The best one-volume edition for general use.

Biography

GILCHRIST, ALEXANDER. *Life of William Blake.* 2 vols. London, 1863.
The pioneering work, still valuable.
WILSON, MONA. *The Life of William Blake.* 2nd ed. London, 1948.
The standard modern life.

Criticism

BEER, J. B. *Blake's Humanism.* Manchester, 1968.
————. *Blake's Visionary Universe.* London, 1969.
BRONOWSKI, J. *William Blake and the Age of Revolution.* New York, 1965.
DAMON, S. FOSTER. *William Blake: His Philosophy and Symbols.* Boston, 1924.
The first attempt to make sense of Blake's work as a whole.
ERDMAN, DAVID V. *Blake: Prophet Against Empire.* Princeton, 1954.
Blake as surreptitious social critic.
FRYE, NORTHRUP, ed. *Blake: A Collection of Critical Essays.* Englewood Cliffs, New Jersey, 1966.
Essays by various critics.
————. *Fearful Symmetry.* Princeton, 1947.
More sophisticated than Damon.
GLECKNER, ROBERT F. *The Piper and the Bard.* Detroit, 1959.
The *Songs of Innocence and of Experience.*
LISTER, RAYMOND. *William Blake.* London, 1968.
MARGOLIOUTH, H. M. *William Blake.* Oxford, 1951.
Perhaps the best introduction.
OSTRIKER, ALICIA. *Vision and Verse in William Blake.* Madison, Wisconsin, 1965.

PALEY, MORTON. *Energy and the Imagination.* London, 1969.
PERCIVAL, M. O. *William Blake's Circle of Destiny.* New York, 1937.

WILLIAM BECKFORD (1759–1844)

Edition

CHAPMAN, GUY. *Vathek.* Cambridge, 1929.

Biography

BROCKMAN, H. A. N. *The Caliph of Fonthill.* London, 1956.

ROBERT BURNS (1759–1796)

Editions

FERGUSON, J. DE LANCEY. *Letters.* 2 vols. Oxford, 1931.
KINSLEY, JAMES. *Poems and Songs.* 3 vols. Oxford, 1968.
  A one-volume edition has been issued.
WESTON, JOHN C. *Selections.* Indianapolis, Indiana, 1968.
  Unusually full and well annotated.

Biography

FERGUSON, J. DE LANCEY. *Pride and Passion.* New York, 1939.
FITZHUGH, ROBERT TYSON. *Robert Burns, His Associates and Contemporaries.* Chapel Hill, North Carolina, 1943.
SNYDER, FRANKLIN BLISS. *The Life of Robert Burns.* New York, 1932.

Criticism

CRAWFORD, THOMAS. *Burns: A Study of the Poems and Songs.* Stanford, California, 1960.
DAICHES, DAVID. *Robert Burns.* New York, 1950.
SNYDER, FRANKLIN BLISS. *Robert Burns: His Personality, His Reputation, and His Art.* Toronto, 1936.

ANN RADCLIFFE (1764–1823)

Editions

DOBRÉE, BONAMY. *The Mysteries of Udolpho.* London, 1966.
GARBER, FREDERICK. *The Italian.* Oxford, 1968.

Biography

GRANT, ALINE. *Ann Radcliffe*. Denver, 1951.

MARIA EDGEWORTH (1767–1849)

Editions

————. *Novels*. 12 vols. London, 1893.
WATSON, GEORGE. *Castle Rackrent*. London, 1964.

Criticism

INGLIS-JONES, ELISABETH. *The Great Maria*. London, 1959.
NEWBY, P. H. *Maria Edgeworth*. London, 1950.

MATTHEW GREGORY LEWIS (1775–1818)

Edition

PECK, LOUIS F. *The Monk*. New York, 1952.

Biography

PECK, LOUIS F. *A Life of Matthew G. Lewis*. Cambridge, Massachusetts, 1961.

The Romantic Period (1800–1830)

BIBLIOGRAPHY

FOGLE, RICHARD HARTER. *Romantic Poets and Prose Writers.* New York, 1967.
Omits the novelists.

HOUTCHENS, CAROLYN WASHBURN, and LAWRENCE HUSTON HOUTCHENS, eds. *The English Romantic Poets and Essayists: A Review of Research and Criticism.* Revised ed. New York, 1966.
Correctly described as a "companion volume to Raysor," this compilation covers Blake, Lamb, Hazlitt, Scott, Southey, Campbell, Thomas Moore, Landor, Leigh Hunt, and De Quincey.

RAYSOR, THOMAS M., ed. *The English Romantic Poets: A Review of Research.* Revised ed. New York, 1956.
A disastrously outmoded introductory chapter (by a scholar now dead) is succeeded by discursive bibliographies by several hands on Wordsworth, Coleridge, Byron, Shelley, and Keats.

"The Romantic Movement: A Selective and Critical Bibliography [1936–   ]." Annually in *ELH: A Journal of English Literary History,* 1937–1949; *Philological Quarterly,* 1950–1964; and *English Language Notes,* 1965–   .
Uneven but indispensable.

LITERARY HISTORY AND CRITICISM

ABRAMS, M. H., ed. *English Romantic Poets: Modern Essays in Criticism.* New York, 1960.

ABRAMS, M. H. *The Mirror and the Lamp: Romantic Theory and the Critical Tradition.* New York, 1953.
Excellent though occasionally daunting.

BATE, WALTER JACKSON. *From Classic to Romantic: Premises of Taste in Eighteenth-Century England.* Cambridge, Massachusetts, 1946.

ELTON, OLIVER. *A Survey of English Literature, 1780–1830.* 2 vols. London, 1912.
Old-fashioned, but elegantly written.

FRYE, NORTHROP. *A Study of English Romanticism.* New York, 1968.
Concise, brilliant, readable, arguable.

GLECKNER, ROBERT F., and GERALD E. ENSCOE, eds. *Romanticism: Points of View.* Englewood Cliffs, New Jersey, 1962.
An extremely useful collection of essays by various writers

from Walter Pater to Earl R. Wasserman, including A. O. Lovejoy's famous and indispensable essay on the subject.

HOUGH, GRAHAM. *The Romantic Poets*. London, 1953.

JACK, IAN. *English Literature, 1815–1832*. (*Oxford History of English Literature,* vol. X.) Oxford, 1963.

KROEBER, KARL. *Romantic Narrative Art*. Madison, Wisconsin, 1960.

RENWICK, W. L. *English Literature, 1789–1815*. (*Oxford History of English Literature,* vol. IX.) Oxford, 1963.

POLITICAL, SOCIAL, AND INTELLECTUAL HISTORY

WATSON, J. STEVEN. *The Reign of George III, 1760–1815*. (*Oxford History of England,* vol. XII.) Oxford, 1960.

WILLEY, BASIL. *Nineteenth-Century Studies*. New York, 1949.

WOODWARD, SIR LLEWELLYN. *The Age of Reform, 1815–1870*. (*Oxford History of England,* vol. XIII.) 2nd ed. Oxford, 1962.

COLLECTIONS

BUCKLER, WILLIAM E. *Nineteenth-Century Fiction: Minor Classics*. 2 vols. Boston, 1967.

HAYWARD, JOHN. *The Oxford Book of Nineteenth-Century Verse*. Oxford, 1964.

PERKINS, DAVID. *English Romantic Writers*. New York, 1967.
Twenty writers are represented and fully annotated. Both prose and poetry are included.

WOODRING, CARL. *Prose of the Romantic Period*. Boston, 1961.

WILLIAM WORDSWORTH (1770–1850)

Editions

BUTT, JOHN. *Selected Poetry and Prose*. London, 1964.
An excellent selection.

DE SELINCOURT, E. *Letters of William and Dorothy Wordsworth*. 6 vols. Oxford, 1935–1939.

DE SELINCOURT, E., and HELEN DARBISHIRE. *Poetical Works*. 5 vols. Oxford, 1940–1949.
Excludes *The Prelude*.

DE SELINCOURT, E. *The Prelude*. Revised ed., by Helen Darbishire. Oxford, 1959.

STILLINGER, JACK. *Selected Poems and Prefaces*. Boston, 1965.
  An excellent selection, with very good notes.
ZALL, PAUL M. *Literary Criticism*. Lincoln, Nebraska, 1966.

Biography

MOORMAN, MARY C. *Wordsworth: A Biography*. 2 vols. Oxford,
  1957–1966.
  Definitive.

Criticism

ABERCROMBIE, LASCELLES. *The Art of Wordsworth*. London, 1952.
  Originally a series of lectures delivered in 1935.
BATESON, F. W. *Wordsworth: A Re-interpretation*. 2nd ed. London,
  1956.
CLARKE, C. C. *Romantic Paradox*. New York, 1962.
DAVIS, JACK, ed. *Discussions of William Wordsworth*. Boston, 1964.
  Essays by various critics.
FERRY, DAVID. *The Limits of Mortality*. Middletown, Connecticut,
  1959.
  On the major poems, including *The Prelude*.
HARTMAN, GEOFFREY H. *Wordsworth's Poetry, 1787–1814*. New
  Haven, 1964.
  Superb.
HAVENS, RAYMOND DEXTER. *The Mind of a Poet*. 2 vols. Baltimore,
  1941.
  The second volume is a commentary on *The Prelude*.
JONES, JOHN. *The Egotistical Sublime: A History of Wordsworth's
  Imagination*. London, 1954.
PERKINS, DAVID. *Wordsworth and the Poetry of Sincerity*. Cam-
  bridge, Massachusetts, 1964.
WOODRING, CARL. *Wordsworth*. Boston, 1965.
  A specially useful introductory guide to the poetry.

SIR WALTER SCOTT (1771–1832)

Editions

GRIERSON, H. J. C., et al. *Letters*. 12 vols. London, 1932–1937.
LANG, ANDREW. *Complete Poetical Works*. 6 vols. Boston, 1902.
———. *The Waverley Novels*. 48 vols. London, 1892–1894.

Biography

JOHNSON, EDGAR. *The Great Unknown: The Life of Sir Walter Scott*.
  London, 1969.

LOCKHART, J. G. *Memoirs of the Life of Sir Walter Scott, Bart.* 10 vols. Edinburgh, 1839.

> One of the great biographies in the language.

Criticism

COCKSHUT, A. O. J. *The Achievement of Sir Walter Scott.* New York, 1969.

DAVIE, DONALD *The Heydey of Sir Walter Scott.* New York, 1961.

HART, F. R. *Scott's Novels.* Charlottesville, Virginia, 1966.

> Outstanding.

HILLHOUSE, J. T. *The Waverley Novels and Their Critics.* Minneapolis, 1936.

WELSH, ALEXANDER. *The Hero of the Waverley Novels.* London, 1963.

SAMUEL TAYLOR COLERIDGE (1772–1834)

Editions

COBURN, KATHLEEN. *Collected Edition of the Works.* London, 1969–   .

> In progress.

———. *Notebooks.* New York, 1957–   .

> In progress.

COLERIDGE, E. H. *Complete Poetical Works.* 2 vols. Oxford, 1912.

GRIGGS, EARL LESLIE. *Collected Letters.* Oxford, 1956–   .

> In progress.

RAYSOR, THOMAS M. *Shakespearean Criticism.* 2 vols. Cambridge, Massachusetts, 1930.

RICHARDS, I. A. *The Portable Coleridge.* New York, 1950.

WATSON, GEORGE. *Biographia Literaria.* London, 1956.

Biography

CHAMBERS, E. K. *Samuel Taylor Coleridge.* 2nd ed. Oxford, 1950.

Criticism

APPLEYARD, J. A. *Coleridge's Philosophy of Literature.* Cambridge, Massachusetts, 1965.

BATE, WALTER JACKSON. *Coleridge.* London, 1969.

BEER, J. B. *Coleridge the Visionary.* London, 1959.

FOGLE, RICHARD HARTER. *The Idea of Coleridge's Criticism.* Berkeley, 1962.

House, Humphry. *Coleridge*. London, 1953.
Clear, economical, and sane.

Lowes, John Livingston. *The Road to Xanadu*. 2nd ed. Boston, 1930.
The most compelling and important single work of Coleridge criticism, though perhaps it is not criticism.

Richards, I. A. *Coleridge on Imagination*. London, 1934.
On the *Biographia Literaria*.

Schneider, Elisabeth. *Coleridge, Opium, and Kubla Khan*. Chicago, 1953.

Schulz, Max F. *The Poetic Voices of Coleridge*. Detroit, 1963.

Suther, Marshall Edward. *Visions of Xanadu*. New York, 1965.

ROBERT SOUTHEY (1774–1843)

Editions

Fitzgerald, M. H. *Poems*. London, 1909.
———. *Letters*. London, 1912.
Supplemented by *New Letters,* ed. Kenneth Curry (New York, 1965).

Biography and Criticism

Carnall, Geoffrey. *Robert Southey and His Age*. Oxford, 1960.
Simmons, Jack. *Southey*. London, 1945.

JANE AUSTEN (1775–1817)

Editions

Chapman, R. W. *Letters*. 2nd ed. Oxford, 1952.
———. *The Novels*. 5 vols. 3rd ed. Oxford, 1933.
The definitive edition, now completed by *Volume VI: Minor Works* (1954).

Biography

Jenkins, Elizabeth. *Jane Austen*. New York, 1949.

Criticism

Babb, Howard S. *Jane Austen's Novels: The Fabric of Dialogue*. Columbus, Ohio, 1962.

LASCELLES, MARY. *Jane Austen and Her Art*. Oxford, 1939.

LITZ, A. WALTON. *Jane Austen*. New York, 1965.

> An excellent introduction to the novels.

MUDRICK, MARVIN. *Jane Austen: Irony as Defense and Discovery*. Princeton, 1952.

> Notorious but indispensable.

SOUTHAM, B. C., ed. *Jane Austen: The Critical Heritage*. London, 1968.

> Contemporary and near-contemporary reviews of individual works.

WATT, IAN, ed. *Jane Austen: A Collection of Critical Essays*. Englewood Cliffs, New Jersey, 1963.

> Essays by various critics.

WRIGHT, ANDREW. *Jane Austen: A Study in Structure*. Revised ed. London, 1961.

CHARLES LAMB (1775–1834)

Editions

BROWN, JOHN MASON. *The Portable Charles Lamb*. New York, 1949.

> A good selection with a useful introduction.

LUCAS, E. V. *Letters*. 3 vols. London, 1935.

———. *Works*. London, 1912.

TILLYARD, E. M. W. *Lamb's Criticism: A Selection*. Cambridge, 1923.

Biography and Criticism

BARNETT, GEORGE L. *Charles Lamb: The Evolution of Elia*. Bloomington, Indiana, 1964.

BLUNDEN, EDMUND. *Charles Lamb and His Contemporaries*. Cambridge, 1933.

> Mainly biographical.

LUCAS, E. V. *Life of Charles Lamb*. 2nd ed. London, 1921.

WALTER SAVAGE LANDOR (1775–1864)

Editions

CHAMBERS, E. K. *Poetry and Prose*. Oxford, 1946.

> A selection.

WELBY, T. E., and STEPHEN WHEELER. *Complete Works*. 16 vols. London, 1927–1936.

Biography and Criticism

ELWIN, MALCOLM. *Landor*. London, 1958.
SUPER, R. H. *Walter Savage Landor*. New York, 1954.

WILLIAM HAZLITT (1778–1830)

Editions

HOWE, P. P. *Complete Works*. 21 vols. London, 1930–1934.
KEYNES, GEOFFREY. *Selected Essays*. London, 1930.

Biography and Criticism

BAKER, HERSCHEL. *William Hazlitt*. Cambridge, Massachusetts, 1962.
   The best single introduction.
HOWE, P. P. *The Life of William Hazlitt*. 3rd ed. London, 1947.
SCHNEIDER, ELISABETH. *The Aesthetics of William Hazlitt*. Philadelphia, 1933.

THOMAS MOORE (1779–1852)

Editions

DOWDEN, W. S. *Letters*. 2 vols. Oxford, 1964.
GODLEY, A. D. *Poetical Works*. London, 1910.

Biography

JONES, H. M. *The Harp that Once*. New York, 1937.

LEIGH HUNT (1784–1859)

Editions

HOUTCHENS, LAWRENCE HUSTON, and CAROLYN WASHBURN
   HOUTCHENS. *Dramatic Criticism*. New York, 1949.
   Followed by *Literary Criticism* (1956) and *Political and Occasional Essays* (1962).
MILFORD, H. S. *Poetical Works*. London, 1923.
MORPURGO, J. E. *Autobiography*. New York, 1949.

Biography and Criticism

BLUNDEN, EDMUND. *Leigh Hunt and His Circle.* New York, 1930.
STOUT, G. D. *The Political History of Leigh Hunt's 'Examiner.'* St. Louis, 1949.

THOMAS DE QUINCEY (1785–1859)

Editions

DOBRÉE, BONAMY. *Thomas De Quincey.* New York, 1965.
    Selections.
MASSON, DAVID. *Collected Writings.* 14 vols. London, 1896–1897.
TAVE, STUART M. *New Essays.* Princeton, 1966.

Biography

EATON, HORACE A. *Thomas De Quincey: A Biography.* New York, 1936.
JORDAN, JOHN E. *De Quincey to Wordsworth: A Biography of a Relationship.* Berkeley, 1962.
SACKVILLE-WEST, EDWARD. *A Flame in Sunlight: The Life and Work of De Quincey.* London, 1936.
    American title: *Thomas De Quincey, His Life and Work.*

Criticism

GOLDMAN, ALBERT. *The Mine and the Mint.* Carbondale, Illinois, 1965.
    A source study.
JORDAN, JOHN E. *Thomas De Quincey, Literary Critic.* Berkeley, 1952.
PROCTOR, S. K. *Thomas De Quincey's Theory of Literature.* Ann Arbor, 1943.

THOMAS LOVE PEACOCK (1785–1866)

Editions

BRETT-SMITH, H. F. B., and C. E. JONES. *Works.* 10 vols. London, 1924–1934.
GARNETT, DAVID. *Novels.* London, 1948.

Biography and Criticism

DAWSON, CARL. *Thomas Love Peacock*. London, 1968.

MILLS, HOWARD. *Peacock: His Circle and His Age*. Cambridge, 1969.

PRIESTLEY, J. B. *Thomas Love Peacock*. Revised ed. London, 1966.

VAN DOREN, CARL. *The Life of Thomas Love Peacock*. London, 1911.

GEORGE NOEL GORDON, LORD BYRON (1788–1824)

Editions

COLERIDGE, E. H., and R. E. PROTHERO. *Works*. 13 vols. London, 1898–1904.

QUENNELL, PETER. *Byron: A Self-Portrait: Letters and Diaries*. 2 vols. London, 1950.

————. *Selections from Poetry, Letters, and Journals*. London, 1949.

SMITH, D. NICHOL. *Poetry and Prose*. Oxford, 1940.
  A useful selection.

Biography

MARCHAND, LESLIE A. *Byron: A Biography*. 3 vols. New York, 1957.
  The definitive biography.

Criticism

GLECKNER, ROBERT F. *Byron and the Ruins of Paradise*. Baltimore, 1967.

LOVELL, ERNEST J. *Byron: The Record of a Quest*. Austin, Texas, 1949.

MARCHAND, LESLIE A. *Byron's Poetry*. Boston, 1965.

MARSHALL, W. H. *The Structure of Byron's Major Poems*. Philadelphia, 1962.

RUTHERFORD, ANDREW. *Byron: A Critical Study*. Stanford, California, 1962.

WEST, PAUL. *Byron and the Spoiler's Art*. New York, 1960.

————, ed. *Byron: A Collection of Critical Essays*. Englewood Cliffs, New Jersey, 1963.
  Essays by various critics.

PERCY BYSSHE SHELLEY (1792–1822)

Editions

HOLLOWAY, JOHN. *Selected Poems.* London, 1960.

HUTCHINSON, THOMAS. *Complete Poetical Works.* New York, 1951.

INGPEN, ROGER, and W. E. PECK. *Complete Works.* 10 vols. New York, 1926–1930.

JONES, FREDERICK L. *Letters.* 2 vols. Oxford, 1964.

MATTHEWS, G. M. *Selected Poems and Prose.* Oxford, 1964.
A good selection with a useful introduction.

Biography

BLUNDEN, EDMUND. *Shelley: A Life Story.* New York, 1947.

CAMERON, KENNETH NEILL. *The Young Shelley: Genesis of a Radical.* London, 1951.

WHITE, NEWMAN IVEY. *Shelley.* 2nd ed. 2 vols. New York, 1947.
A condensation of the first edition was issued in one volume in 1945.

Criticism

BAKER, CARLOS. *Shelley's Major Poetry.* Princeton, 1948.

FOGLE, RICHARD HARTER. *The Imagery of Keats and Shelley.* Chapel Hill, North Carolina, 1949.

KING-HELE, DESMOND. *Shelley: The Man and the Poet.* New York, 1960.
A study of the poetry in a biographical context.

RIDENOUR, GEORGE M., ed. *Shelley: A Collection of Critical Essays.* Englewood Cliffs, New Jersey, 1965.
Essays by various critics.

ROGERS, NEVILLE. *Shelley at Work.* Oxford, 1956.

WASSERMAN, EARL. *The Subtler Language.* Baltimore, 1959.
Close and intelligent readings of a number of poems, including "Adonais." A separately issued reading of "Prometheus Unbound" appeared in 1965.

JOHN KEATS (1795–1821)

Editions

BUSH, DOUGLAS. *Selected Poems and Letters.* Boston, 1959.
The best one-volume selection.

GARROD, H. W. *Poetical Works*. 2nd ed. Oxford, 1958.
ROLLINS, HYDER EDWARD. *The Keats Circle*. 2 vols. 2nd ed. Cambridge, Massachusetts, 1965.
————. *Letters*. 2 vols. Cambridge, Massachusetts, 1958.
SHARROCK, ROGER. *Selected Poems and Letters*. Oxford, 1964.
A good selection, with a useful introduction.
TRILLING, LIONEL. *Selected Letters*. New York, 1951.

Biography

BATE, WALTER JACKSON. *John Keats*. Cambridge, Massachusetts, 1963.
Definitive.
————, ed. *Keats: A Collection of Critical Essays*. Englewood Cliffs, New Jersey, 1964.
Essays by various critics.
BUSH, DOUGLAS. *John Keats*. London, 1967.
Biography and criticism.
GARROD, H. W. *Keats*. 2nd ed. Oxford, 1939.
GITTINGS, ROBERT. *John Keats: The Living Year: September 1818 to September 1819*. Cambridge, Massachusetts, 1954.
————. *John Keats*. London, 1968.
JONES, JOHN. *John Keats's Dream of Truth*. London, 1969.
WARD, AILEEN. *Keats: The Making of a Poet*. London, 1963.

Criticism

BATE, WALTER JACKSON, ed. *Keats: A Collection of Critical Essays*. Englewood Cliffs, New Jersey, 1964.
Essays by various critics.
FINNEY, CLAUDE LEE. *The Evolution of Keats' Poetry*. 2 vols. Cambridge, Massachusetts, 1936.
Consideration of the poems in a biographical context.
FOGLE, RICHARD HARTER. *The Imagery of Keats and Shelley*. Chapel Hill, North Carolina, 1949.
RIDLEY, M. R. *Keats' Craftsmanship*. 2nd ed. London, 1963.
WASSERMAN, EARL R. *The Finer Tone: Keats' Major Poems*. Baltimore, 1953.
A series of excellent readings of the major poems.

The Victorian Age (1830-1890)

BIBLIOGRAPHY

BUCKLEY, JEROME HAMILTON. *Victorian Poets and Prose Writers.* New York, 1966.
> Omits the novelists except those (Meredith and Hardy) who are also poets.

FAVERTY, FREDERIC E., ed. *The Victorian Poets: A Guide to Research.* 2nd ed. Cambridge, Massachusetts, 1968.
> Discursive bibliographies by several hands on all the major and a number of minor poets.

STEVENSON, LIONEL, ed. *Victorian Fiction: A Guide to Research.* Cambridge, Massachusetts, 1964.
> Discursive bibliographies by several hands on Disraeli, Bulwer-Lytton, Dickens, Thackeray, Trollope, the Brontës, Mrs. Gaskell, Kingsley, Collins, Reade, George Eliot, Meredith, Hardy, George Moore, and Gissing.

"Victorian Bibliography [1932–   ]." Annually in *Modern Philology,* 1933–1957, and *Victorian Studies,* 1958–   .
> Uneven but indispensable. Convenient collections of issues have been published twice under the title *Bibliographies of Studies in Victorian Literature* (1945, ed. William D. Templeman, and 1956, ed. Austin Wright).

LITERARY HISTORY AND CRITICISM

BUCKLEY, JEROME HAMILTON. *The Victorian Temper.* Cambridge, Massachusetts, 1951.

ELTON, OLIVER. *A Survey of English Literature, 1830–1880.* 2 vols. London, 1920.
> Old-fashioned, but elegantly written.

LEVINE, GEORGE, and WILLIAM MADDEN, eds. *The Art of Victorian Prose.* New York, 1968.
> Essays by various critics.

WRIGHT, AUSTIN, ed. *Victorian Literature: Modern Essays in Criticism.* New York, 1961.
> Essays by various critics.

POLITICAL, SOCIAL, AND INTELLECTUAL HISTORY

BRIGGS, ASA. *The Age of Improvement.* London, 1962.

ENSOR, R. C. K. *England, 1870–1914.* (*Oxford History of England,* vol. XIV.) Oxford, 1936.

HOUGHTON, WALTER E. *The Victorian Frame of Mind, 1830–1870.*
New Haven, 1957.
THOMSON, DAVID. *England in the Nineteenth Century.* Baltimore,
1950.
A specially lucid introduction.
WOODWARD, SIR LEWELLYN. *The Age of Reform, 1815–1870.* (*Oxford History of England,* vol. XIII.) 2nd ed. Oxford, 1962.
YOUNG, G. M. *Victorian England.* New York, 1936.

COLLECTIONS

BUCKLER, WILLIAM E. *Nineteenth-Century Fiction: Minor Classics.*
2 vols. Boston, 1967.
————. *Prose of the Victorian Period.* Boston, 1958.
BUCKLEY, JEROME HAMILTON. *The Pre-Raphaelites.* New York,
1968.
BUCKLEY, JEROME HAMILTON, and GEORGE BENJAMIN WOODS,
eds. *Poetry of the Victorian Period.* Chicago, 1965.
HAYWARD, JOHN. *The Oxford Book of Nineteenth-Century Verse.*
Oxford, 1964.
HARROLD, CHARLES FREDERICK, and WILLIAM D. TEMPLEMAN.
English Prose of the Victorian Era. New York, 1938.
A generous selection, with perhaps the best short introduction
to the Victorian period.
HOUGHTON, WALTER E., and G. ROBERT STANGE. *Victorian Poetry
and Poetics.* Boston, 1968.
WOODS, GEORGE BENJAMIN. *Poetry of the Victorian Period.* Revised
ed. by Jerome Hamilton Buckley. Chicago, 1955.

THOMAS CARLYLE (1795–1881)

Editions

ALTICK, RICHARD D. *Past and Present.* Boston, 1965.
HARROLD, CHARLES FREDERICK. *Sartor Resartus.* New York, 1937.
TENNYSON, GEORGE B. *Selections.* New York, 1968.
TRAILL, H. D. *Works.* 30 vols. London, 1896–1899.

Biography and Criticism

HARROLD, CHARLES FREDERICK. *Carlyle and German Thought.* New
Haven, 1934.
LAVALLEY, ALBERT J. *Carlyle and the Idea of the Modern.* New
Haven, 1968.

NEFF, EMERY. *Carlyle.* New York, 1932.
SYMONS, JULIAN. *Carlyle: The Life and Ideas of a Prophet.* New York, 1952.
TENNYSON, GEORGE B. *Sartor Called Resartus.* Princeton, 1965.
  A critical study of *Sartor Resartus.*

THOMAS BABINGTON MACAULAY (1800–1859)

Editions

————. *Works.* 9 vols. London, 1905–1907.
YOUNG, G. M. *Prose and Poetry.* London, 1952.

Biography and Criticism

BRYANT, ARTHUR. *Macaulay.* New York, 1933.
TREVELYAN, GEORGE OTTO. *The Life and Letters of Lord Macaulay.* London, 1876.
  By his nephew.

JOHN HENRY NEWMAN (1801–1890)

Editions

BLEHL, VINCENT FERRER. *The Essential Newman.* New York, 1963.
CULLER, A. DWIGHT. *Apologia Pro Vita Sua.* Boston, 1956.
DESSAIN, CHARLES STEPHEN, and VINCENT FERRER BLEHL. *Letters and Diaries.* Edinburgh, 1961–   .
  In progress.
TILLOTSON, GEOFFREY. *Prose and Poetry.* London, 1957.

Biography

HARROLD, CHARLES FREDERICK. *John Henry Newman: An Expository and Critical Study of His Mind, Thought, and Art.* New York, 1945.
  Perhaps the best single introduction to the man and his work.
TREVOR, MERIOL. *Newman.* 2 vols. London, 1962.
  The first volume is subtitled *The Pillar of the Cloud,* the second volume, *Light in Winter.* A Roman Catholic view.

Criticism

CULLER, A. DWIGHT. *The Imperial Intellect.* New Haven, 1955.
HOUGHTON, WALTER E. *The Art of Newman's Apologia.* New Haven, 1945.

ELIZABETH BARRETT BROWNING (1806–1861)

Editions

————. *Poetical Works*. Oxford, 1904.
PORTER, CHARLOTTE, and HELEN A. CLARKE. *Complete Works*. 6
   vols. New York, 1900.

Biography

TAPLIN, GARDNER B. *The Life of Elizabeth Barrett Browning*. New
   Haven, 1957.

Criticism

HAYTER, ALETHEA. *Mrs. Browning: A Poet's Work in Its Setting*.
   London, 1962.

JOHN STUART MILL (1806–1873)

Editions

COSS, J. J. *Autobiography*. New York, 1944.
PRIESTLEY, F. E. L., et al. *Collected Works*. Toronto, 1963–
   In progress.
WARNOCK, MARY. *On Liberty* [et al.]. London, 1962.

Biography

PACKE, MICHAEL ST. JOHN. *The Life of John Stuart Mill*. London,
   1954.

Criticism

ANSCHUTZ, R. P. *The Philosophy of J. S. Mill*. Oxford, 1953.
ELLERY, JOHN B. *John Stuart Mill*. New York, 1954.

EDWARD FITZGERALD (1809–1883)

Editions

COHEN, J. M. *Letters*. London, 1960.
RICHARDSON, JOANNA. *Selected Works*. London, 1962.
WEBER, CARL J. *FitzGerald's Rubaiyat*. Waterville, Maine, 1959.
   The best edition for scholarly purposes.

Biography and Criticism

TERHUNE, ALFRED M. *The Life of Edward FitzGerald.* New Haven, 1947.

ALFRED, LORD TENNYSON (1809–1892)

Editions

BUCKLEY, JEROME HAMILTON. *Poems.* Boston, 1958.
Splendidly annotated.
MILLGATE, MICHAEL. *Selected Poems.* Oxford, 1963.
RICKS, CHRISTOPHER. *The Poems.* London, 1969.
TENNYSON, HALLAM. *Works.* 9 vols. London, 1907–1908.

Biography

TENNYSON, CHARLES. *Alfred Tennyson.* London, 1949.
The standard life.

Criticism

BUCKLEY, JEROME HAMILTON. *Tennyson: The Growth of a Poet.* Cambridge, Massachusetts, 1960.
JUMP, JOHN D., ed. *Tennyson: The Critical Heritage.* New York, 1967.
Contemporary and near-contemporary views of individual works, together with extracts from general critiques.
KILLHAM, JOHN, ed. *Critical Essays on the Poetry of Tennyson.* London, 1960.
Essays by various critics.
MARSHALL, GEORGE O., JR. *A Tennyson Handbook.* New York, 1963.
Useful for information on individual poems.

WILLIAM MAKEPEACE THACKERAY (1811–1863)

Editions

RAY, GORDON N. *Letters and Private Papers.* 4 vols. Cambridge, Massachusetts, 1945–1946.
SAINTSBURY, GEORGE. *Works.* 17 vols. Oxford, 1908.
TILLOTSON, GEOFFREY, and KATHLEEN TILLOTSON. *Vanity Fair.* Boston, 1963.
Definitive.

Biography

RAY, GORDON N. *Thackeray, the Uses of Adversity, 1811–1846.*
New York, 1955.
Followed—and concluded—by *Thackeray, the Age of Wisdom, 1847–1863* (1958). Definitive.

Criticism

RAY, GORDON N. *The Buried Life.* Cambridge, Massachusetts, 1952.
STEVENSON, LIONEL. *The Showman of Vanity Fair.* New York, 1947.
TILLOTSON, GEOFFREY. *Thackeray the Novelist.* Cambridge, 1954.
TILLOTSON, GEOFFREY, and DONALD HAWES, eds. *Thackeray: The Critical Heritage.* London, 1968.
Contemporary and near-contemporary views, mainly the responses to the novels as they were published.
WELSH, ALEXANDER, ed. *Thackeray: A Collection of Critical Essays.* Englewood Cliffs, New Jersey, 1968.
Essays by various critics.

ROBERT BROWNING (1812–1889)

Editions

KENYON, F. G. *Works.* 10 vols. London, 1912.
NOWELL-SMITH, SIMON. *Poetry and Prose.* Cambridge, Massachusetts, 1951.
SMALLEY, DONALD. *Poems.* Boston, 1956.

Biography

GRIFFIN, W. H., and H. C. MINCHIN. *The Life of Robert Browning.* 3rd ed. London, 1938.
MILLER, BETTY. *Browning: A Portrait.* London, 1952.

Criticism

DE VANE, WILLIAM CLYDE. *A Browning Handbook.* 2nd ed. New York, 1955.
A gold mine.
DREW, PHILIP, ed. *Robert Browning: A Collection of Critical Essays.* Boston, 1966.
Essays by various critics.

HONAN, PARK. *Browning's Characters*. New Haven, 1961.
KING, ROMA A. *The Bow and the Lyre*. Ann Arbor, 1957.
LANGBAUM, ROBERT. *The Poetry of Experience*. New York, 1957.
LITZINGER, BOYD, and K. L. KNICKERBOCKER, eds. *The Browning Critics*. Louisville, Kentucky, 1965.
   A considerable collection of critical essays by various hands.
RAYMOND, WILLIAM O. *The Infinite Moment*. 2nd ed. Toronto, 1965.

CHARLES DICKENS (1812–1870)

Editions

————. *New Oxford Illustrated Dickens*. 21 vols. Oxford, 1947–1958.
   Being superseded by the Tillotson edition.
HOUSE, MADELINE, and GRAHAM STOREY. *Letters*. 1965–   .
   The definitive edition, in progress.
TILLOTSON, KATHLEEN, et al. *The Clarendon Dickens*. Oxford, 1966–   .
   The definitive edition, in progress.

Biography

JOHNSON, EDGAR. *Charles Dickens*. 2 vols. New York, 1952.
   Standard.
NISBET, ADA. *Dickens and Ellen Ternan*. Berkeley, 1952.

Criticism

COCKSHUT, A. O. J. *The Imagination of Charles Dickens*. New York, 1961.
FIELDING, K. J. *Charles Dickens*. London, 1958.
FORD, GEORGE H. *Dickens and His Readers*. Princeton, 1955.
FORD, GEORGE H., and LAURIAT LANE, JR., eds. *The Dickens Critics*. Ithaca, New York, 1961.
   Essays by various critics.
GARIS, ROBERT. *The Dickens Theatre: A Reassessment of the Novels*. Oxford, 1965.
HOUSE, HUMPHRY. *The Dickens World*. London, 1941.
MILLER, J. HILLIS. *Charles Dickens: The World of His Novels*. Cambridge, Massachusetts, 1958.

ANTHONY TROLLOPE (1815–1882)

Editions

BOOTH, BRADFORD A. *Letters.* New York, 1951.

SADLEIR, MICHAEL. *The Barsetshire Novels.* 14 vols. Oxford, 1929.

SADLEIR, MICHAEL, and FREDERICK PAGE. *The Oxford Trollope.* 15 vols. Oxford, 1948–1954.
Ultimately abandoned.

Biography and Criticism

BOOTH, BRADFORD A. *Anthony Trollope.* Bloomington, Indiana, 1958.
Comprehensive.

COCKSHUT, A. O. J. *Anthony Trollope.* London, 1955.
Emphasizes the "dark" Trollope.

GEROULD, WINIFRED GREGORY, and JAMES THAYER GEROULD. *A Guide to Trollope.* Princeton, 1948.
Quirky.

SADLEIR, MICHAEL. *Trollope: A Commentary.* 3rd ed. London, 1945.
Still in some respects the best introduction.

SMALLEY, DONALD, ed. *Trollope: The Critical Heritage.* New York, 1969.
Contemporary and near-contemporary reviews of individual works.

CHARLOTTE BRONTË (1816–1855) and EMILY BRONTË (1818–1848)

Editions

HATFIELD, C. W. *Complete Poems of Emily Brontë.* New York, 1941.

JACK, JANE, and MARGARET SMITH. *Jane Eyre.* Oxford, 1969.
The first volume in the projected "Clarendon Edition" of the novels.

WISE, T. J., and J. A. SYMINGTON. *The Shakespeare Head Brontë.* 19 vols. Oxford, 1932–1938.

Biography and Criticism

GASKELL, ELIZABETH C. *Life of Charlotte Brontë.* 2 vols. New York, 1857.

GÉRIN, WINIFRED. *Charlotte Brontë*. Oxford, 1967.
HANSON, LAWRENCE, and ELIZABETH HANSON. *The Four Brontës*. London, 1949.
RATCHFORD, FANNY E. *The Brontës' Web of Childhood*. New York, 1941.

ARTHUR HUGH CLOUGH (1819–1861)

Editions

LOWRY, H. F., et al. *Poems*. Oxford, 1951.
MULHAUSER, FREDERICK L. *Correspondence*. 2 vols. Oxford, 1957.
TRAWICK, BUCKNER B. *Selected Prose Works*. University, Alabama, 1964.

Biography and Criticism

CHORLEY, KATHARINE. *Arthur Hugh Clough: The Uncommitted Mind*. Oxford, 1962.
HOUGHTON, WALTER E. *The Poetry of Clough: An Essay in Revaluation*. New Haven, 1963.

GEORGE ELIOT (MARY ANN EVANS, 1819–1880)

Editions

————. *Writings*. 25 vols. Boston, 1908.
BEATY, JEROME. *Middlemarch from Notebook to Novel*. Urbana, Illinois, 1960.
HAIGHT, GORDON S. *Letters*. 7 vols. New Haven, 1954–1955.

Biography

HAIGHT, GORDON S. *George Eliot: A Biography*. New York, 1968.

Criticism

HARDY, BARBARA, ed. *Middlemarch: A Critical Approach*. New York, 1968.
    Essays by various critics.
HARDY, BARBARA. *The Novels of George Eliot*. London, 1959.
HARVEY, W. J. *The Art of George Eliot*. London, 1961.
KNOEPFLMACHER, U. C. *George Eliot's Early Novels*. Berkeley, 1968.
    Scenes of Clerical Life, Adam Bede, The Mill on the Floss.
THALE, JEROME. *The Novels of George Eliot*. New York, 1959.

JOHN RUSKIN (1819–1900)

Editions

CLARK, KENNETH. *Ruskin Today.* New York, 1964.
Selections.
COOK, E. T., and ALEXANDER WEDDERBURN. *Works.* 39 vols. London, 1903–1912.
Standard.
EVANS, JOAN, and JOHN HOWARD WHITEHOUSE. *Diaries.* 3 vols. Oxford, 1956–1959.
QUENNELL, PETER. *Selected Writings.* London, 1952.
ROSENBERG, JOHN D. *The Genius of John Ruskin.* New York, 1963.
Selections.

Biography

EVANS, JOAN. *John Ruskin.* London, 1954.
LEON, DERRICK. *Ruskin: The Great Victorian.* London, 1949.

Criticism

LADD, HENRY. *The Victorian Morality of Art.* New York, 1932.
ROSENBERG, JOHN D. *The Darkening Glass.* New York, 1962.

MATTHEW ARNOLD (1822–1888)

Editions

————. *Works.* 15 vols. London, 1903–1904.
ALLOTT, KENNETH. *Poems.* London, 1965.
Well annotated.
CULLER, A. DWIGHT. *Poetry and Criticism.* Boston, 1961.
The best one-volume edition, with good notes.
SUPER, R. H. *Complete Prose Works.* Ann Arbor, 1960–
The definitive edition, in progress.

Biography and Criticism

BROWN, E. K. *Matthew Arnold: A Study in Conflict.* Chicago, 1948.
CULLER, A. DWIGHT. *Imaginative Reason: The Poetry of Matthew Arnold.* New Haven, 1966.
JOHNSON, W. STACY. *The Voices of Matthew Arnold.* New Haven, 1961.

TRILLING, LIONEL. *Matthew Arnold.* 2nd ed. London, 1955.
The best full-scale treatment.

GEORGE MEREDITH (1828–1909)

Editions

————. *Works.* 36 vols. London, 1914.
CLINE, C. L. *Collected Letters.* 3 vols. Oxford, 1968.
HOUGH, GRAHAM. *Selected Poems.* London, 1962.

Biography

STEVENSON, LIONEL. *The Ordeal of George Meredith.* New York, 1953.

Criticism

KELVIN, NORMAN. *A Troubled Eden.* Stanford, California, 1961.
SASSOON, SIEGFRIED. *Meredith.* London, 1948.
TREVELYAN, GEORGE MACAULAY. *The Poetry and Philosophy of George Meredith.* London, 1912.
WRIGHT, WALTER F. *Art and Substance in George Meredith.* Lincoln, Nebraska, 1953.

DANTE GABRIEL ROSSETTI (1828–1882)

Editions

DOUGHTY, OSWALD. *Poems.* London, 1957.
DOUGHTY, OSWALD, and JOHN ROBERT WAHL. *Letters.* 4 vols. Oxford, 1965–   .
In progress.

Biography and Criticism

DOUGHTY, OSWALD. *A Victorian Romantic.* 2nd ed. London, 1960.
FLEMING, G. H. *Rossetti and the Pre-Raphaelite Brotherhood.* London, 1967.

CHRISTINA ROSSETTI (1830–1894)

Edition

ROSSETTI, W. M. *Poetical Works.* London, 1904.

Biography and Criticism

PACKER, LONA MOSK. *Christina Rossetti.* Berkeley, 1963.
SHOVE, FREDEGOND. *Christina Rossetti.* Cambridge, 1931.

LEWIS CARROLL (CHARLES LUTWIDGE DODGSON, 1832–1898)

Editions

————. *Complete Works.* New York, 1936.
GREEN, R. LANCELYN. *Diaries.* New York, 1954.

Biography and Criticism

GREEN, R. LANCELYN. *The Story of Lewis Carroll.* New York, 1950.
WILLIAMS, S. H. and F. MADAN. *The Lewis Carroll Handbook.* New York, 1962.

WILLIAM MORRIS (1834–1896)

Editions

BRIGGS, ASA. *Selected Writings and Designs.* London, 1962.
COLE, G. D. H. *Stories in Prose, Stories in Verse, Shorter Poems, Lectures and Essays.* London, 1948.
HENDERSON, PHILIP. *Letters.* London, 1950.
MORRIS, MAY. *Collected Works.* 24 vols. London, 1910–1915.

Biography and Criticism

ARNOT, ROBERT P. *William Morris: The Man and the Myth.* New York, 1964.
GRENNAN, MARGARET B. *William Morris: Medievalist and Revolutionary.* New York, 1945.
MORRIS, MAY. *William Morris.* 2 vols. Oxford, 1936.

ALGERNON CHARLES SWINBURNE (1837–1909)

Editions

BINYON, LAURENCE. *Selected Poems.* Oxford, 1939.
GOSSE, EDMUND, and THOMAS J. WISE. *Complete Works.* 20 vols. London, 1925–1927.

LANG, CECIL Y. *Letters.* 6 vols. New Haven, 1959–1962.
WILSON, EDMUND. *The Novels.* New York, 1962.

Biography

CASSIDY, JOHN A. *Algernon C. Swinburne.* New York, 1964.
FULLER, JEAN OVERTON. *Swinburne: A Critical Biography.* London, 1969.

Criticism

CONNOLLY, THOMAS E. *Swinburne's Theory of Poetry.* Albany, New York, 1964.
HYDER, CLYDE K. *Swinburne's Literary Career and Fame.* Durham, North Carolina, 1933.
PETERS, ROBERT L. *The Crowns of Apollo: Swinburne's Principles of Literature and Art.* Detroit, 1965.

WALTER PATER (1839–1894)

Editions

————. *Works.* 10 vols. London, 1910.
ALDINGTON, RICHARD. *Selected Works.* London, 1948.
CLARK, KENNETH. *The Renaissance.* London, 1961.

Biography and Criticism

CECIL, Lord DAVID. *Walter Pater.* Cambridge, 1955.
JOHNSON, R. V. *Walter Pater: A Study of His Critical Outlook.* Melbourne, 1961.
MCKENZIE, GORDON. *The Literary Character of Walter Pater.* Berkeley, 1967.

The Early Modern Period (1890–1920)

LITERARY HISTORY

FRASER, G. S. *The Modern Writer and His World.* Revised ed. New York, 1965.

STEWART, J. I. M. *Eight Modern Writers. (Oxford History of English Literature,* vol. XII.) Oxford, 1963.
   Hardy, James, Shaw, Conrad, Kipling, Yeats, Joyce, and Lawrence.

TINDALL, WILLIAM YORK. *Forces in Modern British Literature.* New York, 1956.

POLITICAL, SOCIAL, AND INTELLECTUAL HISTORY

ENSOR, R. C. K. *England, 1870–1914. (Oxford History of England,* vol. XIV.) Oxford, 1936.

WHITEHEAD, ALFRED NORTH. *Science and the Modern World.* New York, 1925.

THOMAS HARDY (1840–1928)

Editions

———. *Collected Poems.* 2nd ed. London, 1930.

———. *Works.* Revised ed. 24 vols. London, 1912–1931.

RANSOM, JOHN CROWE. *Selected Poems.* New York, 1961.

Biography

HARDY, FLORENCE E. *The Early Life of Thomas Hardy, 1840–91.* London, 1928.

———. *The Later Years, 1892–1928.* London, 1930.

WEBER, CARL J. *Hardy of Wessex.* 2nd ed. New York, 1965.
   Definitive.

Criticism

GUÉRARD, ALBERT J. *Thomas Hardy.* Cambridge, Massachusetts, 1949.

———, ed. *Hardy: A Collection of Critical Essays.* Englewood Cliffs, New Jersey, 1963.
   Essays by various critics.

HYNES, SAMUEL L. *The Pattern of Hardy's Poetry.* Chapel Hill, North Carolina, 1961.

MORRELL, ROY. *Thomas Hardy.* Kuala Lumpur, 1965.

PINION, F. B. *A Hardy Companion.* London, 1968.

RUTLAND, WILLIAM R. *Thomas Hardy: A Study of His Writings.* Oxford, 1938.

WEBSTER, HARVEY CURTIS. *On a Darkling Plain.* Chicago, 1947.

GERARD MANLEY HOPKINS (1844–1889)

Editions

ABBOTT, C. C. *Letters.* 2nd ed. 3 vols. London, 1955–1956.

GARDNER, W. H. *Poems.* 4th ed. New York, 1967.

PICK, JOHN. *A Hopkins Reader.* Oxford, 1953.

Biography and Criticism

BOYLE, ROBERT. *Metaphor in Hopkins.* Chapel Hill, North Carolina, 1961.

GARDNER, W. H. *Gerard Manley Hopkins.* 2 vols. London, 1944–1949.

The first volume appeared in a revised edition in 1948.

HARTMAN, GEOFFREY, ed. *Hopkins: A Collection of Critical Essays.* Englewood Cliffs, New Jersey, 1966.

Essays by various critics.

HEUSER, ALAN. *The Shaping Vision of Gerard Manley Hopkins.* London, 1958.

KENYON CRITICS. *Gerard Manley Hopkins.* New York, 1945.

A collection of essays by Robert Lowell, F. R. Leavis, and others.

PETERS, W. A. M. *Gerard Manley Hopkins.* London, 1948.

ROBERT LOUIS STEVENSON (1850–1894)

Editions

———. *Works.* 26 vols. London, 1922–1923.

PRITCHETT, V. S. *Novels and Stories.* London, 1945.

SMITH, JANET ADAM. *Collected Poems.* London, 1950.

Biography and Criticism

DAICHES, DAVID. *Robert Louis Stevenson.* Norfolk, Connecticut, 1947.

FURNAS, J. C. *Voyage to Windward: The Life of Robert Louis Stevenson.* London, 1952.

KIELY, ROBERT. *Robert Louis Stevenson and the Fiction of Adventure.* Cambridge, Massachusetts, 1964.

OSCAR WILDE (1854–1900)

Editions

————. *Works.* 14 vols. London, 1908.

ELLMANN, RICHARD. *Selected Writings.* London, 1961.
    An excellent selection.

HART-DAVIS, RUPERT. *Letters.* New York, 1962.

HOLLAND, VYVYAN. *Complete Works.* New ed. London, 1966.
    Comprehensive.

Biography and Criticism

ELLMANN RICHARD, ed. *Oscar Wilde: A Collection of Critical Essays.* Englewood Cliffs, New Jersey, 1969.
    Essays by various critics.

ERVINE, ST. JOHN. *Oscar Wilde.* London, 1951.

JULLIAN, PHILIPPE. *Oscar Wilde.* New York, 1969.

RODITI, EDOUARD. *Oscar Wilde.* Norfolk, Connecticut, 1947.

SAN JUAN, EPIFANIO. *The Art of Oscar Wilde.* Princeton, 1967.

WOODCOCK, GEORGE. *The Paradox of Oscar Wilde.* New York, 1950.

GEORGE BERNARD SHAW (1856–1950)

Editions

————. *Collected Works.* 31 vols. London, 1930–1932.

————. *Complete Prefaces.* London, 1965.

————. *Complete Plays.* London, 1965.

LAURENCE, DAN H. *Collected Letters.* London, 1965–
    In progress.

————. *Selected Non-Dramatic Writings.* Boston, 1965.

Biography

BROWN, IVOR. *Shaw in His Time.* London, 1965.

ERVINE, ST. JOHN. *Bernard Shaw.* New York, 1956.

Criticism

BENTLEY, ERIC. *George Bernard Shaw*. 2nd ed. London, 1967.
A highly regarded critical study.

KAUFMAN, R. J., ed. *Shaw: A Collection of Critical Essays*. Englewood Cliffs, New Jersey, 1965.
Essays by various critics.

MEISEL, MARTIN. *Shaw and the Nineteenth-Century Theatre*. Princeton, 1963.

JOSEPH CONRAD (1857–1924)

Editions

————. *Works*. 22 vols. London, 1923–1928.

ZABEL, MORTON DAUWEN. *The Portable Conrad*. New York, 1947.

Biography

BAINES, JOCELYN. *Joseph Conrad*. London, 1960.

JEAN-AUBRY, GERARD. *The Sea Dreamer*. London, 1957.

Criticism

CURLE, RICHARD. *Joseph Conrad and His Characters*. London, 1957.

GUÉRARD, ALBERT J. *Conrad the Novelist*. Cambridge, Massachusetts, 1958.
Excellent.

HAY, ELOISE KNAPP. *The Political Novels of Joseph Conrad*. Chicago, 1963.

HEWITT, DOUGLAS. *Conrad: A Reassessment*. Cambridge, 1952.

KARL, FREDERICK R. *A Reader's Guide to Joseph Conrad*. New York, 1960.

MOSER, THOMAS. *Joseph Conrad: Achievement and Decline*. Cambridge, Massachusetts, 1957.

MUDRICK, MARVIN, ed. *Conrad: A Collection of Critical Essays*. Englewood Cliffs, New Jersey, 1966.
Essays by various critics.

PALMER, JOHN A. *Joseph Conrad's Fiction: A Study in Literary Growth*. Ithaca, New York, 1968.

STALLMAN, R. W., ed. *The Art of Joseph Conrad*. East Lansing, Michigan, 1960.
Another collection by various critics.

A. E. HOUSMAN (1859–1936)

Editions

CARTER, JOHN. *Collected Poems.* New York, 1965.
————. *Selected Prose.* Cambridge, 1961.

Biography and Criticism

GOW, A. S. F. *Housman: A Sketch.* Cambridge, 1936.
HOUSMAN, LAURENCE. *AEH.* London, 1937.
RICHARDS, GRANT. *Housman.* London, 1941.
RICKS, CHRISTOPHER, ed. *A. E. Housman: A Collection of Critical Essays.* Englewood Cliffs, New Jersey, 1968.
   Essays by various critics.
WATSON, GEORGE. *A. E. Housman: A Divided Life.* London, 1957.
WITHERS, PERCY. *A Buried Life.* London, 1940.

FRANCIS THOMPSON (1859–1907)

Editions

CONNOLLY, TERENCE L. *Literary Criticism.* New York, 1948.
   A second volume was issued in 1959.
————. *Poems.* Revised ed. New York, 1941.

Biography and Criticism

MEYNELL, EVARARD. *The Life of Francis Thompson.* 2nd ed. London, 1926.
MEYNELL, VIOLA. *Francis Thompson and Wilfrid Meynell.* London, 1952.
REID, J. C. *Francis Thompson: Man and Poet.* London, 1959.
THOMSON, PAUL VAN KUYKENDALL. *Francis Thompson.* New York, 1961.

RUDYARD KIPLING (1865–1936)

Editions

————. *Works.* 31 vols. London, 1913–1938.
BEECROFT, JOHN. *Kipling: A Selection of His Stories and Poems.* 2 vols. Garden City, New York, 1956.
ELIOT, T. S. *A Choice of Kipling's Verse.* London, 1951.

Biography

CARRINGTON, CHARLES. *The Life of Rudyard Kipling.* New York, 1955.

Criticism

BODELSEN, C. A. *Aspects of Kipling's Art.* Manchester, 1964.

BROWN, HILTON. *Rudyard Kipling.* London, 1945.

DOBRÉE, BONAMY. *Rudyard Kipling, Realist and Fabulist.* London, 1967.

GILBERT, ELLIOTT L., ed. *Kipling and the Critics.* New York, 1965. Essays by various critics.

RUTHERFORD, ANDREW, ed. *Kipling's Mind and Art.* London, 1964. Another collection by various critics.

TOMPKINS, J. M. S. *The Art of Rudyard Kipling.* London, 1959.

H. G. WELLS (1866–1946)

Edition

——. *Collected Works.* 28 vols. London, 1924–1927.

Biography and Criticism

BELGION, MONTGOMERY. *H. G. Wells.* Revised ed. London, 1964.

BERGONZI, BERNARD. *The Early H. G. Wells: A Study of the Scientific Romances.* Toronto, 1961.

BROME, VINCENT. *H. G. Wells: A Biography.* London, 1951.

DICKSON, LOVAT. *H. G. Wells: His Turbulent Life and Times.* New York, 1969.

HILLEGAS, MARK R. *The Future as Nightmare: H. G. Wells and the Anti-Utopians.* New York, 1967.

ARNOLD BENNETT (1867–1931)

Editions

——. *The Arnold Bennett Omnibus Book.* London, 1931. Contains *Riceyman Steps, Elsie and the Child, Lord Raingo,* and *Accident.*

——. *The Clayhanger Family.* London, 1925. Contains *Clayhanger, Hilda Lessways,* and *These Twain.*

————. *The Penguin Arnold Bennett.* 6 vols. London, 1954.
Contains five of the novels, together with selections from the *Journal.*
————. *Journal.* 3 vols. New York, 1932–1933.
HEPBURN, JAMES. *Letters.* New York, 1966–   .
In progress.

Biography

POUND, REGINALD. *Arnold Bennett.* London, 1952.

Criticism

ALLEN, WALTER. *Arnold Bennett.* Denver, 1949.
HALL, JAMES. *Arnold Bennett: Primitivism and Taste.* Seattle, 1959.
HEPBURN, JAMES. *The Art of Arnold Bennett.* Bloomington, Indiana, 1963.

ERNEST DOWSON (1867–1900)

Editions

FLOWER, DESMOND, and HENRY MAAS. *Letters.* London, 1967.
LONGAKER, MARK. *Poems.* Philadelphia, 1963.

Biography and Criticism

LONGAKER, MARK. *Ernest Dowson.* 3rd ed. Philadelphia, 1967.
SWANN, THOMAS B. *Ernest Dowson.* New York, 1965.

JOHN GALSWORTHY (1867–1933)

Editions

————. *Works.* 30 vols. London, 1923–1926.
WEST, ANTHONY. *The Galsworthy Reader.* New York, 1967.

Biography and Criticism

BARKER, DUDLEY. *The Man of Principle.* London, 1963.
MARROT, HAROLD V. *Life and Letters.* New York, 1936.

JOHN MILLINGTON SYNGE (1871–1909)

Editions

HENN, T. R. *Plays and Poems.* London, 1963.

SKELTON, ROBIN, et al. *Collected Works.* Oxford, 1962–
    The definitive edition, in progress.

Biography and Criticism

GERSTENBERGER, DONNA. *John Millington Synge.* New York, 1964.
GREENE, DAVID H., and EDWARD M. STEPHENS. *J. M. Synge.* New
    York, 1959.
    The best single work on Synge.
PRICE, ALAN. *Synge and Anglo-Irish Drama.* London, 1961.

The Recent Past (1920–1960)

LITERARY HISTORY

DAICHES, DAVID. *The Present Age in British Literature.* Bloomington, Indiana, 1958.

A broad and lucid survey followed by extensive bibliographies.

FRASER, G. S. *The Modern Writer and His World.* Revised ed. New
York, 1965.

STEWART, J. I. M. *Eight Modern Writers.* (*Oxford History of English Literature,* vol. XII.) Oxford, 1963.

Hardy, James, Shaw, Conrad, Kipling, Yeats, Joyce, and Lawrence.

TINDALL, WILLIAM YORK. *Forces in Modern British Literature.* New
York, 1956.

POLITICAL, SOCIAL, AND INTELLECTUAL HISTORY

TAYLOR, A. J. P. *English History, 1914–1945.* (*Oxford History of
England,* vol. XV.) Oxford, 1965.

WHITEHEAD, ALFRED NORTH. *Science and the Modern World.* New
York, 1925.

WILLIAM BUTLER YEATS (1865–1939)

Editions

––––––. *Autobiography.* New York, 1953.

––––––. *Collected Plays.* New ed. New York, 1953.

––––––. *Collected Poems.* 2nd ed. New York, 1950.

––––––. *Essays and Introductions.* New York, 1961.

ALLT, PETER, and RUSSELL K. ALSPACH. *The Variorum Edition of
the Poems.* New York, 1957.

ALSPACH, RUSSELL K., and CATHERINE C. ALSPACH. *The Variorum
Edition of the Plays.* New York, 1966.

WADE, ALLAN. *Letters.* New York, 1955.

Biography

HONE, JOSEPH. *W. B. Yeats.* 2nd ed. London, 1962.

Criticism

ELLMANN, RICHARD. *The Identity of Yeats.* New York, 1954.

––––––. *Yeats: The Man and the Masks.* Revised ed. New York,
1961.

JEFFARES, A. NORMAN. *A Commentary on the Collected Poems of W. B. Yeats.* Stanford, California, 1968.
KERMODE, FRANK. *Romantic Image.* London, 1957.
A seminal work, of the first importance.
STAUFFER, DONALD A. *The Golden Nightingale.* New York, 1949.
STOCK, A. G. *W. B. Yeats: His Poetry and Thought.* Cambridge, 1961.
UNTERECKER, JOHN. *A Reader's Guide to William Butler Yeats.* New York, 1959.
Extremely useful.
————, ed. *Yeats: A Collection of Critical Essays.* Englewood Cliffs, New Jersey, 1963.
Essays by various critics.

E. M. FORSTER (1879–   )

Editions

————. *Abinger Harvest.* London, 1936.
A collection of essays. A second volume, *Two Cheers for Democracy,* was issued in 1951.
————. *Aspects of the Novel.* London, 1927.
The influential Clark Lectures.
————. *Collected Tales.* New York, 1947.
————. *Howards End.* London, 1910.
————. *The Longest Journey.* London, 1907.
————. *A Passage to India.* London, 1924.
————. *A Room with a View.* London, 1908.
————. *Where Angels Fear to Tread.* London, 1905.

Biography and Criticism

BRADBURY, MALCOLM, ed. *Forster: A Collection of Critical Essays.* Englewood Cliffs, New Jersey, 1966.
Essays by various critics.
CREWS, FREDERICK C. *E. M. Forster.* Oxford, 1962.
STONE, WILFRID. *The Cave and the Mountain.* Stanford, California, 1966.
Contains much biographical information.
TRILLING, LIONEL. *E. M. Forster.* Norfolk, Connecticut, 1943.
WILDE, ALAN. *Art and Order.* New York, 1964.

SEAN O'CASEY (1880–1964)

Editions

————. *Autobiographies.* 2 vols. London, 1963.
————. *Collected Plays.* 4 vols. New York, 1957–1959.
ATKINSON, BROOKS. *The Sean O'Casey Reader: Plays, Autobiographies, Opinions.* New York, 1968.
    An excellent selection.

Biography and Criticism

FALLON, GABRIEL. *Sean O'Casey, the Man I Knew.* Boston, 1965.
KRAUSE, DAVID. *Sean O'Casey, the Man and His Work.* New York, 1960.

JAMES JOYCE (1882–1941)

Editions

————. *Finnegans Wake.* New York, 1939.
————. *Ulysses.* New York, 1934.
GILBERT, STUART. *Letters.* New York, 1957.
LEVIN, HARRY. *The Portable James Joyce.* New York, 1947.
    A generous selection, including *Dubliners* and *A Portrait of the Artist,* essays, and poetry. Richard Ellmann has edited the definitive edition of *A Portrait of the Artist* (New York, 1968).
MASON, ELLSWORTH, and RICHARD ELLMANN. *Critical Writings.* London, 1959.
SCHOLES, ROBERT. *Dubliners.* London, 1967.
    Standard.

Biography and Criticism

ADAMS, ROBERT MARTIN. *Surface and Symbol: The Consistency of James Joyce's Ulysses.* New York, 1962.
ELLMANN, RICHARD. *James Joyce.* New York, 1959.
    The definitive biography.
GIFFORD, DON. *Notes for Joyce.* New York, 1968.
    A guide to *Dubliners* and *A Portrait of the Artist as a Young Man.*
KENNER, HUGH. *Dublin's Joyce.* London, 1955.
LEVIN, HARRY. *James Joyce: A Critical Introduction.* Revised ed. Norfolk, Connecticut, 1960.

STALEY, THOMAS F., ed. *James Joyce Today: Essays on the Major Works.* Bloomington, Indiana, 1966.
Essays by various critics.
TINDALL, WILLIAM YORK. *A Reader's Guide to James Joyce.* New York, 1959.

VIRGINIA WOOLF (1882–1941)

Editions

——. *Works.* 16 vols. London, 1929–1952.
WOOLF, LEONARD. *Collected Essays.* 4 vols. London, 1966, 1967.

Biography and Criticism

BENNETT, JOAN. *Virginia Woolf.* Cambridge, 1945.
BLACKSTONE, BERNARD. *Virginia Woolf.* New York, 1949.
LEASKA, MITCHELL A. *Virginia Woolf's Lighthouse.* New York, 1970.
WOOLF, LEONARD. *Growing.* New York, 1962.
The important second volume of compelling autobiography by Virginia Woolf's widower. The other volumes are also of much interest, though they deal less centrally with Virginia Woolf.

D. H. LAWRENCE (1885–1930)

Editions

——. *Works.* 22 vols. London, 1945–1960.
DE SOLA PINTO, VIVIAN, and WARREN ROBERTS. *Complete Poems.* 2 vols. London, 1964.
MOORE, HARRY T. *A D. H. Lawrence Miscellany.* Carbondale, Illinois, 1959.
TRILLING, DIANA. *The Portable D. H. Lawrence.* New York, 1947.

Biography

MOORE, HARRY T. *The Intelligent Heart.* 2nd ed. New York, 1960.
NEHLS, EDWARD. *D. H. Lawrence: A Composite Biography.* 3 vols. Madison, Wisconsin, 1957–1959.

Criticism

DRAPER, RONALD P. *D. H. Lawrence.* New York, 1964.
HOFFMAN, FREDERICK J., and HARRY T. MOORE, eds. *The Achievement of D. H. Lawrence.* Norman, Oklahoma, 1953.
Essays by various critics.

LEAVIS, F. R. *D. H. Lawrence, Novelist*. London, 1955.

MOORE, HARRY T. *A Reader's Guide to D. H. Lawrence*. 2nd ed. New York, 1964.

MOYNAHAN, JULIAN. *The Deed of Life: The Novels and Tales of Lawrence*. Princeton, 1963.

SPILKA, MARK, ed. *D. H. Lawrence: A Collection of Critical Essays*. Englewood Cliffs, New Jersey, 1963.
Essays by various critics.

VIVAS, ELISEO. *D. H. Lawrence*. Evanston, Illinois, 1960.

RUPERT BROOKE (1887–1915)

Editions

HASSALL, CHRISTOPHER. *Prose*. London, 1956.

KEYNES, GEOFFREY. *Letters*. London, 1968.

———. *Poetical Works*. London, 1963.

Biography and Criticism

HASSALL, CHRISTOPHER. *Rupert Brooke*. New York, 1964.

JOYCE CARY (1888–1957)

Editions

———. *Novels*. 16 vols. London, 1951–1959.

———. *Spring Song*. London, 1960.
Short stories.

Biography and Criticism

MAHOOD, M. M. *Joyce Cary's Africa*. Boston, 1965.
Authoritative.

WOKENFELD, JACK. *Joyce Cary: The Developing Style*. New York, 1968.

WRIGHT, ANDREW. *Joyce Cary: A Preface to His Novels*. New York, 1958.

KATHERINE MANSFIELD (1888–1923)

Edition

———. *Collected Stories*. London, 1945.

Biography and Criticism

ALPERS, ANTONY. *Katherine Mansfield.* London, 1954.
  Biography.
DALY, SARALYN R. *Katherine Mansfield.* New York, 1965.

WILFRED OWEN (1893–1918)

Edition

DAY LEWIS, CECIL. *Collected Poems.* London, 1963.
OWEN, HAROLD, and JOHN BELL. *Collected Letters.* London, 1968.

Criticism

WELLAND, D. S. R. *Wilfred Owen: A Critical Study.* London, 1960.

ALDOUS HUXLEY (1894–1963)

Editions

————. *Collected Criticism.* New York, 1960.
————. *Collected Essays.* New York, 1960.
————. *Collected Short Stories.* New York, 1956.
————. *Collected Works.* 26 vols. London, 1947–1964.
SMITH, GROVER. *Letters.* London, 1969.

Criticism

ATKINS, JOHN. *Aldous Huxley.* Revised ed. London, 1967.
BOWERING, PETER. *Aldous Huxley: A Study of the Major Novels.*
  London, 1968.
MECKIER, JEROME. *Aldous Huxley: Satire and Structure.* London,
  1969.

ROBERT GRAVES (1895–   )

Edition

————. *Collected Poems.* London, 1965.

Biography and Criticism

DAY, DOUGLAS. *Swifter than Reason.* Chapel Hill, North Carolina,
  1963.
KIRKHAM, MICHAEL. *The Poetry of Robert Graves.* London, 1969.

GEORGE ORWELL (ERIC ARTHUR BLAIR, 1903–1950)

Editions

ORWELL, SONIA, and IAN ANGUS. *Collected Essays, Journalism, and Letters.* 4 vols. London, 1968.
ROVERE, RICHARD H. *The Orwell Reader.* New York, 1956.

Biography and Criticism

ALLDRITT, KEITH. *The Making of George Orwell.* London, 1969.
BRANDER, LAURENCE. *George Orwell.* London, 1954.
HOLLIS, CHRISTOPHER. *A Study of George Orwell.* London, 1956.
REES, RICHARD. *George Orwell, Fugitive from the Camp of Victory.* Carbondale, Illinois, 1962.
WOODCOCK, GEORGE. *The Crystal Spirit: A Study of George Orwell.* Boston, 1966.
    Excellent.

EVELYN WAUGH (1903–1966)

Editions

————. *A Little Learning: An Autobiography.* Boston, 1964.
ROLO, CHARLES J. *The World of Evelyn Waugh.* Boston, 1958.

Biography and Criticism

CARENS, JAMES F. *The Satiric Art of Evelyn Waugh.* Seattle, 1966.
STOPP, FREDERICK J. *Evelyn Waugh: Portrait of an Artist.* Boston, 1958.

C. DAY LEWIS (1904–   )

Editions

————. *The Buried Day.* London, 1960.
————. *Collected Poems.* London, 1954.

Criticism

DYMENT, CLIFFORD. *C. Day Lewis.* London, 1955.

GRAHAM GREENE (1904–   )

Editions

———. *Collected Essays*. London, 1969.
———. *Works*. London, 1959–   .
In progress.

Biography and Criticism

ALLOTT, KENNETH, and MIRIAM FARRIS. *The Art of Graham Greene*. London, 1951.
ATKINS, JOHN. *Graham Greene*. Revised ed. London, 1966.
DEVITIS, A. A. *Graham Greene*. New York, 1964.
LODGE, DAVID. *Graham Greene*. New York, 1966.

SAMUEL BECKETT (1906–   )

Editions

———. *Endgame*. New York, 1958.
———. *Happy Days*. New York, 1961.
———. *Krapp's Last Tape and Other Dramatic Pieces*. New York, 1960.
———. *Malloy, Malone Dies, and The Unnameable*. New York, 1959.
———. *Waiting for Godot*. New York, 1954.
CALDER, JOHN. *A Samuel Beckett Reader*. London, 1967.
A sampling of a number of his works.

Biography and Criticism

COE, RICHARD N. *Samuel Beckett*. New York, 1964.
COHN, RUBY. *Samuel Beckett*. New Brunswick, New Jersey, 1962.
ESSLIN, MARTIN, ed. *Samuel Beckett: A Collection of Critical Essays*. Englewood Cliffs, New Jersey, 1965.
Essays by various critics.
FLETCHER, JOHN. *The Novels of Samuel Beckett*. New York, 1964.
———. *Samuel Beckett's Art*. London, 1967.
KENNER, HUGH. *Samuel Beckett, a Critical Study*. New York, 1962.

W. H. AUDEN (1907–   )

Editions

———. *Collected Longer Poems*. London, 1968.

————. *Collected Shorter Poems, 1927–57*. London, 1966.
Followed by *About the House* (1966) and *City Without Walls* (1969).
————. *The Dyer's Hand and Other Essays*. New York, 1962.

Criticism

FULLER, JOHN. *A Reader's Guide to W. H. Auden*. London, 1970.
GREENBERG, HERBERT. *Quest for the Necessary: W. H. Auden and the Dilemma of Divided Consciousness*. Cambridge, Massachusetts, 1968.
HOGGART, RICHARD. *Auden: An Introductory Essay*. London, 1951.
SPEARS, MONROE K., ed. *Auden: A Collection of Critical Essays*. Englewood Cliffs, New Jersey, 1964.
    Essays by various critics.
————. *The Poetry of Auden: The Disenchanted Island*. New York, 1963.
    Outstanding.

LOUIS MACNEICE (1907–1963)

Edition

————. *Collected Poems*. London, 1963.

Criticism

PRESS, JOHN. *Louis MacNeice*. London, 1965.

STEPHEN SPENDER (1909–   )

Editions

————. *Selected Poems*. New York, 1964.
————. *World Within World*. London, 1951.
    Autobiography.

WILLIAM GOLDING (1911–   )

Editions

————. *The Brass Butterfly: A Play*. London, 1958.
————. *Free Fall*. New York, 1959.
————. *The Hot Gates and Other Occasional Pieces*. London, 1965.
————. *The Inheritors*. New York, 1955.
————. *Lord of the Flies*. London, 1954.
————. *Pincher Martin*. New York, 1956.

————. *The Pyramid*. London, 1967.
————. *The Spire*. New York, 1964.

Criticism

KINKEAD-WEEKES, MARK, and IAN GREGOR. *William Golding*. London, 1967.

LAWRENCE DURRELL (1912–   )

Editions

————. *The Alexandria Quartet*. London, 1962.
————. *Collected Poems*. London, 1960.
————. *Nunquam*. New York, 1970.
————. *Tunc*. London, 1968.

Biography and Criticism

FRASER, G. S. *Lawrence Durrell*. London, 1968.

DYLAN THOMAS (1914–1953)

Editions

————. *Collected Poems*. Norfolk, Connecticut, 1952.
FITZGIBBON, CONSTANTINE. *Selected Letters*. London, 1966.

Biography

ACKERMAN, JOHN. *Dylan Thomas: His Life and Work*. London, 1964.
    Dylan Thomas as Welsh.
FITZGIBBON, CONSTANTINE. *The Life of Dylan Thomas*. London, 1965.

Criticism

COX, C. B., ed. *Dylan Thomas: A Collection of Critical Essays*. Englewood Cliffs, New Jersey, 1966.
    Essays by various critics.
MAUD, RALPH. *Entrances to Dylan Thomas' Poetry*. Pittsburgh, 1963.
MOYNIHAN, WILLIAM T. *The Craft and Art of Dylan Thomas*. Ithaca, New York, 1966.
OLSON, ELDER. *The Poetry of Dylan Thomas*. Chicago, 1954.

American Literature

General

GUIDES TO LITERARY STUDY

BLANCK, JACOB. *Bibliography of American Literature.* New Haven, 1955– . Five volumes (*Henry Adams* through *Longfellow*) have appeared.

A meticulously compiled bibliography of greater interest to the advanced student and bibliophile than to the novice. Excludes writers who died after 1930.

SPILLER, ROBERT E., et al. *Literary History of the United States.* 3rd ed. 2 vols. New York, 1963.

The standard history, together with the standard bibliography, both of great usefulness; can be supplemented by the "MLA International Bibliography," published annually in *PMLA* ("Publications of the Modern Language Association of America") and by *American Literary Scholarship: An Annual* (Durham, North Carolina, 1965 et seq.).

GOHDES, CLARENCE. *Bibliographical Guide to the Study of the Literature of the U.S.A.* 2nd ed. Durham, North Carolina, 1963.

Excellent.

JONES, HOWARD MUMFORD. *Guide to American Literature and Backgrounds Since 1890.* 3rd ed. Cambridge, Massachusetts, 1964.

Wonderfully comprehensive for the period covered.

LEARY, LEWIS. *Articles on American Literature, 1900–1950.* Durham, North Carolina, 1954.

An indispensable guide to periodical essays.

STOVALL, FLOYD. *Eight American Authors: A Review of Research and Criticism.* New York, 1956.

Reprinted with *Bibliographical Supplement, 1955–62* (1963). Usefully selective and critical: Poe, Emerson, Hawthorne, Thoreau, Melville, Whitman, Mark Twain, Henry James.

REFERENCE WORKS

BURKE, W. J., and WILL D. HOWE. *American Authors and Books, 1640 to the Present Day.* Revised by Irving Weiss. New York, 1962.

Less critical and generally less useful than *The Oxford Companion* or *The Reader's Encyclopedia,* but somewhat more comprehensive.

HART, JAMES D. *The Oxford Companion to American Literature.* 4th ed. New York, 1965.

Authors, titles, characters, allusions: comprehensive, deliberately tame, extremely useful.

HERZBERG, MAX J., et al. *The Reader's Encyclopedia of American Literature.* New York, 1962.

Comparable to the *Oxford Companion:* there is not much to choose between them.

LITERARY HISTORY

CUNLIFFE, MARCUS. *The Literature of the United States.* Revised ed. London, 1961.

Crisp, brief, readable.

QUINN, ARTHUR HOBSON, et al. *The Literature of the American People.* New York, 1951.

SPILLER, ROBERT E., et al. *Literary History of the United States.* 3rd ed. 2 vols. New York, 1963.

The standard history, together with the standard bibliography, both of great usefulness.

POLITICAL, SOCIAL, AND INTELLECTUAL HISTORY

CARGILL, OSCAR. *Intellectual America: Ideas on the March.* New York, 1941.

COMMAGER, HENRY STEELE. *The American Mind.* New Haven, 1950.

CURTI, MERLE. *The Growth of American Thought.* 3rd ed. New York, 1964.

MATTHIESSEN, F. O. *American Renaissance.* New York, 1941.

A classic.

MORISON, SAMUEL ELIOT. *The Oxford History of the American People.* New York, 1965.

The best one-volume history.

PERSONS, STOW. *American Minds.* New York, 1958.

SCHLESINGER, ARTHUR M., and DIXON R. FOX, eds. *A History of American Life.* 13 vols. New York, 1927–1948.

Social history.

PARRINGTON, VERNON LOUIS. *Main Currents in American Thought.* 3 vols. New York, 1927–1930.

A classic whose influence is gradually waning.

COLLECTIONS

BRADLEY, SCULLEY, et al. *The American Tradition in Literature.*
2 vols. 3rd ed. New York, 1967.
An unusually full and intelligent anthology.

CHASE, RICHARD. *American Folk Tales and Songs.* New York, 1956.

HART, JAMES D., and CLARENCE GOHDES. *America's Literature.*
New York, 1955.
A good one-volume selection.

LYNN, KENNETH S. *The Comic Tradition in America.* London,
1958.

MATTHIESSEN, F. O. *The Oxford Book of American Verse.* New
York, 1950.

MILLER, PERRY. *The American Puritans: Their Prose and Poetry.*
New York, 1956.

NYE, RUSSEL B., and NORMAN S. GRABO. *American Thought and
Writing.* Boston, 1965–   .
In progress.

PEARCE, ROY HARVEY. *Colonial American Writing.* Revised ed.
New York, 1969.

QUINN, ARTHUR HOBSON. *Representative American Plays.* 7th ed.
New York, 1958.

SIMPSON, CLAUDE M. *The Local Colorists: American Short Stories,
1857–1900.* New York, 1960.

STERN, MILTON, and SEYMOUR L. GROSS. *The Viking Portable
Library American Literature Survey.* Revised ed. 4 vols. New
York, 1968.
Conveniently divided into volumes that can actually be held
in the hand.

WHICHER, GEORGE F. *Poetry of the New England Renaissance,
1790–1890.* New York, 1956.

LANGUAGE

FRANCIS, W. NELSON. *The Structure of American English.* New
York, 1958.

MATHEWS, MITFORD. *The Beginnings of American English.* Chicago, 1931.

MENCKEN, H. L. *The American Language.* 4th ed. New York,
1936. Supplements One and Two. New York, 1945, 1948.
No one should miss this masterful and idiosyncratic work.

FOLKLORE

DORSON, RICHARD. *American Folklore*. Chicago, 1959.
THOMPSON, STITH. *The Folktale*. New York, 1946.

POETRY

ARMS, GEORGE. *The Fields Were Green: A New View of Bryant, Whittier, Holmes, Lowell, and Longfellow*. Stanford, California, 1953.
PEARCE, ROY HARVEY. *The Continuity of American Poetry*. Princeton, 1961.
WAGGONER, HYATT H. *American Poets, from the Puritans to the Present Day*. Boston, 1968.

DRAMA

QUINN, ARTHUR HOBSON. *A History of the American Drama from the Beginning to the Civil War*. New York, 1923.
————. *A History of the American Drama from the Civil War to the Present Day*. Revised ed. New York, 1936.

FICTION

CHASE, RICHARD. *The American Novel and Its Tradition*. Garden City, New York, 1957.
COWIE, ALEXANDER. *The Rise of the American Novel*. New York, 1948.
FIEDLER, LESLIE. *Love and Death in the American Novel*. New York, 1960.
   Idiosyncratic.
GERSTENBERGER, DONNA, and GEORGE HENDRICK. *The American Novel, 1789–1959: A Checklist of Twentieth-Century Criticism*. Denver, 1961.
   Promises more than it performs.
QUINN, ARTHUR HOBSON. *American Fiction: An Historical and Critical Survey*. New York, 1936.
VAN DOREN, CARL. *The American Novel, 1789–1939*. Revised ed. New York, 1940.

CRITICISM

FOERSTER, NORMAN. *American Criticism*. Boston, 1928.
JONES, HOWARD MUMFORD. *The Theory of American Literature.*
2nd ed. Ithaca, New York, 1965.

Colonial and Revolutionary America to 1800

LITERARY AND INTELLECTUAL HISTORY

MILLER, PERRY. *The New England Mind: From Colony to Province.* Cambridge, Massachusetts, 1953.

————. *The New England Mind: The Seventeenth Century.* New York, 1939.

MILLER, PERRY, and THOMAS H. JOHNSON. *The Puritans.* Revised ed. 2 vols. New York, 1963.

SCHNEIDER, HERBERT. *The Puritan Mind.* Ann Arbor, 1958.

TYLER, MOSES COIT. *A History of American Literature, 1607–1765.* 2 vols. New York, 1878.

————. *The Literary History of the American Revolution, 1763–1783.* 2 vols. New York, 1897.

WILLIAM BRADFORD (1590–1657)

Edition

MORISON, SAMUEL ELIOT. *Of Plymouth Plantation.* New York, 1952.

Biography

SMITH, BRADFORD. *Bradford of Plymouth.* Philadelphia, 1952.

ANNE BRADSTREET (ca. 1612–1672)

Edition

HENSLEY, JEANNINE. *Works.* Cambridge, Massachusetts. 1967.

Criticism

PIERCY, JOSEPHINE K. *Anne Bradstreet.* New York, 1965.

EDWARD TAYLOR (ca. 1645–1729)

Editions

JOHNSON, THOMAS H. *Poetical Works.* New York, 1939.
  A selection.

STANFORD, DONALD E. *Poems.* New Haven, 1960.

Biography and Criticism

GRABO, NORMAN S. *Edward Taylor.* New York, 1962.

SAMUEL SEWALL (1652–1730)

Edition

VAN DOREN, MARK. *Diary.* New York, 1927.
 An abridgment.

Biography

CHAMBERLAIN, NATHAN H. *Samuel Sewall.* Boston, 1897.
WINSLOW, OLA E. *Samuel Sewall of Boston.* New York, 1964.

COTTON MATHER (1663–1728)

Edition

MURDOCK, KENNETH B. *Selections.* New York, 1926.

Biography and Criticism

WENDELL, BARRETT. *Cotton Mather.* New York, 1891.

WILLIAM BYRD (1674–1744)

Editions

BOYD, WILLIAM K. *Histories.* Raleigh, North Carolina, 1929.
TINLING, MARION, and LOUIS B. WRIGHT. *Secret Diary . . . 1709–1712.* Richmond, Virginia, 1941.
WOODFIN, MAUDE H. *Another Secret Diary . . . 1739–1741.* Richmond, Virginia, 1942.
WRIGHT, LOUIS B., and MARION TINLING. *The London Diary (1717–1721).* New York, 1958.

Biography

BEATTY, RICHMOND C. *William Byrd.* Boston, 1932.

JONATHAN EDWARDS (1703–1758)

Editions

FAUST, CLARENCE H., and THOMAS H. JOHNSON. *Representative Selections.* Revised ed. New York, 1962.
 The best one-volume selection.

MILLER, PERRY, et al. *Works*. New Haven, 1957– .
The definitive edition, in progress.
WILLIAMS, EDWARD, and EDWARD PARSONS. *Works*. 8 vols. Leeds,
1806–1811. Supplement. 2 vols. 1847.
The most complete of several editions.

Biography and Criticism

ALDRIDGE, A. O. *Jonathan Edwards*. New York, 1964.
DAVIDSON, EDWARD H. *Jonathan Edwards: The Narrative of a
Puritan Mind*. Boston, 1966.
MILLER, PERRY. *Jonathan Edwards*. New York, 1949.
WINSLOW, OLA E. *Jonathan Edwards*. New York, 1940.

BENJAMIN FRANKLIN (1706–1790)

Editions

FARRAND, MAX. *Autobiography*. Berkeley, 1949.
LABAREE, LEONARD W., et al. *Papers*. New Haven, 1959– .
In progress.
NYE, RUSSEL B. *Autobiography and Other Writings*. Boston, 1958.
Convenient.
SMYTH, ALBERT H. *Writings*. 10 vols. New York, 1905–1907.
Standard except where superseded by the Labaree *Papers*.

Biography and Criticism

ALDRIDGE, ALFRED O. *Benjamin Franklin, Philosopher and Man*.
Philadelphia, 1965.
COHEN, I. BERNARD. *Benjamin Franklin: His Contribution to the
American Tradition*. Indianapolis, Indiana, 1953.
GRANGER, BRUCE I. *Benjamin Franklin: An American Man of Let-
ters*. Ithaca, New York, 1964.
KETCHAM, RALPH. *Benjamin Franklin*. New York, 1965.
VAN DOREN, CARL. *Benjamin Franklin*. New York, 1938.

JOHN WOOLMAN (1720–1772)

Editions

GUMMERE, AMELIA M. *Journals and Essays*. New York, 1922.
SCUDDER, VIDA D. *The Journal and Other Writings*. Revised ed.
New York, 1952.

Biography and Criticism

CADY, EDWIN H. *John Woolman.* New York, 1966.
PEARE, CATHERINE OWENS. *John Woolman.* New York, 1954.

ST. JEAN DE CREVÈCOEUR (1735–1813)

Edition

TRENT, WILLIAM P. *Letters from an American Farmer.* New York, 1904.

Biography and Criticism

MITCHELL, JULIA P. *St. Jean de Crèvecoeur.* New York, 1916.

THOMAS PAINE (1737–1809)

Editions

CLARK, HARRY H. *Representative Selections.* New York, 1944.
CONWAY, MONCURE D. *Writings.* 4 vols. New York, 1894–1896. Standard.
FONER, PHILIP S. *Complete Writings.* 2 vols. New York, 1945.

Biography and Criticism

CONWAY, MONCURE D. *The Life of Thomas Paine.* 2 vols. New York, 1892.
WOODWARD, WILLIAM E. *Tom Paine.* New York, 1945.

THOMAS JEFFERSON (1743–1826)

Editions

BOYD, JULIAN P., et al. *Papers.* Princeton, 1950– .
    The definitive edition, in progress.
FORD, PAUL L. *Autobiography.* New York, 1914.
———. *Writings.* 10 vols. New York, 1892–1899.
    Standard, though being superseded by the Princeton Jefferson.
KOCH, ADRIENNE, and WILLIAM PEDEN. *Life and Selected Writings.* New York, 1944.
PADOVER, SAUL K. *The Complete Jefferson.* New York, 1943.
    Omits the correspondence.

Biography and Criticism

KOCH, ADRIENNE. *The Philosophy of Thomas Jefferson*. New York, 1943.

MALONE, DUMAS. *Jefferson and His Time*. Boston, 1948–   .
To be completed in five volumes, of which three have appeared to date.

PHILIP FRENEAU (1752–1832)

Editions

LEARY, LEWIS. *Last Poems*. New Brunswick, New Jersey, 1946.
Supplements the Pattee edition.

MARSH, PHILIP M. *A Freneau Sampler*. New York, 1963.

PATTEE, F. L. *Poems*. 3 vols. Princeton, 1902–1907.

Biography and Criticism

ADKINS, NELSON F. *Philip Freneau*. New York, 1949.

AXELRAD, JACOB. *Philip Freneau*. Austin, Texas, 1967.

LEARY, LEWIS. *That Rascal Freneau*. New Brunswick, New Jersey, 1941.

The Nineteenth Century

LITERARY AND INTELLECTUAL HISTORY

BERTHOFF, WARNER. *The Ferment of Realism: American Literature, 1884–1919.* New York, 1965.

LAWRENCE, D. H. *Studies in Classic American Literature.* New York, 1923.

The celebrated, sometimes notorious, treatment of Franklin, Crèvecoeur, Cooper, Poe, Hawthorne, Melville, and Whitman.

MARTIN, JAY. *Harvests of Change: American Literature, 1865–1914.* Englewood Cliffs, New Jersey, 1967.

MATTHIESSEN, F. O. *American Renaissance.* New York, 1941. A classic.

ZIFF, LARZER. *The American 1890s.* New York, 1966.

See also the works listed under the general headings, pp. 110–114.

WASHINGTON IRVING (1783–1859)

Editions

————. *Works.* 21 vols. New York, 1860–1861.

POCHMAN, HENRY A., et al. *Complete Works.* Madison, Wisconsin, 1969–   .

The definitive edition, of which one volume has appeared.

————. *Representative Selections.* New York, 1934. Convenient.

TRENT, WILLIAM P., and GEORGE S. HELLMAN. *Journals.* 3 vols. Boston, 1919.

Biography and Criticism

HEDGES, WILLIAM L. *Washington Irving: An American Study, 1802–1832.* Baltimore, 1965.

WAGENKNECHT, EDWARD. *Washington Irving: Moderation Displayed.* New York, 1962.

WILLIAM, STANLEY T. *The Life of Washington Irving.* 2 vols. New York, 1935.

JAMES FENIMORE COOPER (1789–1851)

Editions

————. *Works.* 32 vols. New York, 1859–1861.

BEARD, JAMES F. *Letters and Journals.* 4 vols. Cambridge, Massachusetts, 1960, 1965.

SPILLER, ROBERT E. *Representative Selections.* New York, 1936. Nonfiction only.

Biography and Criticism

DEKKER, GEORGE. *James Fenimore Cooper, the American Scott.* New York, 1967.

GROSSMAN, JAMES. *James Fenimore Cooper.* New York, 1949.

RINGE, DONALD A. *James Fenimore Cooper.* New York, 1962.

SPILLER, ROBERT E. *Fenimore Cooper, Critic of His Times.* New York, 1931.

WALKER, WARREN S. *James Fenimore Cooper: An Introduction and Interpretation.* New York, 1962.

WILLIAM CULLEN BRYANT (1794–1878)

Editions

GODWIN, PARKE. *Poetical Works.* 2 vols. New York, 1883.

––––––. *Prose Writings.* 2 vols. New York, 1884.

MCDOWELL, TREMAINE. *Representative Selections.* New York, 1935.
Convenient.

Biography and Criticism

GODWIN, PARKE. *A Biography of William Cullen Bryant.* 2 vols. New York, 1883.

MCLEAN, ALBERT F., JR. *William Cullen Bryant.* New York, 1964.

PECKHAM, H. H. *Gotham Yankee.* New York, 1950.

RALPH WALDO EMERSON (1803–1882)

Editions

ATKINSON, BROOKS. *The Complete Essays and Other Writings.* New York, 1940.
Convenient.

CARPENTER, FREDERIC IVES. *Representative Selections.* New York, 1934.

EMERSON, EDWARD WALDO. *Complete Works.* 12 vols. Boston, 1903–1904.

EMERSON, EDWARD WALDO, and W. E. FORBES. *Journals.* 10 vols. Boston, 1909–1914.

GILMAN, W. H., et al. *Journals and Miscellaneous Notebooks*. Cambridge, Massachusetts, 1961– .

Five volumes have been published to date.

PERRY, BLISS. *The Heart of Emerson's Journals*. New York, 1926. Reprinted in 1958.

RUSK, RALPH L. *Letters*. 6 vols. New York, 1939.

VAN DOREN, MARK. *The Portable Emerson*. New York, 1946.

WHICHER, STEPHEN E., et al. *Works*. Cambridge, Massachusetts, 1959– .

The definitive edition, in progress.

Biography and Criticism

CAMERON, KENNETH W. *Emerson the Essayist*. 2 vols. Raleigh, North Carolina, 1945.

CARPENTER, FREDERIC IVES. *An Emerson Handbook*. New York, 1953.

A convenient guide.

KONVITZ, MILTON R., and STEPHEN E. WHICHER, eds. *Emerson: A Collection of Critical Essays*. Englewood Cliffs, New Jersey, 1962.

Essays by various critics.

PAUL, SHERMAN. *Emerson's Angle of Vision*. Cambridge, Massachusetts, 1952.

PERRY, BLISS. *Emerson Today*. Princeton, 1931.

RUSK, RALPH L. *The Life of Ralph Waldo Emerson*. New York, 1949.

WHICHER, STEPHEN E. *Freedom and Fate*. Philadelphia, 1953.

NATHANIEL HAWTHORNE (1804–1864)

Editions

CHARVAT, WILLIAM, et al. *Centenary Edition*. Columbus, Ohio, 1962– .

The definitive edition, in progress.

COWLEY, MALCOLM. *The Portable Hawthorne*. Revised ed. New York, 1969.

Convenient and authoritative.

LATHROP, GEORGE P. *Complete Works*. 12 vols. Boston, 1883.

Being superseded by the Centenary Hawthorne.

PEARSON, NORMAN HOLMES. *Complete Novels and Selected Tales*. New York, 1937.

A one-volume edition.

STEWART, RANDALL. *The American Notebooks*. New Haven, 1932.
————. *The English Notebooks*. New York, 1941.
WAGGONER, HYATT H. *Nathaniel Hawthorne, Selected Tales and Sketches*. New York, 1950.

Biography and Criticism

ARVIN, NEWTON. *Hawthorne*. Boston, 1929.
CANTWELL, ROBERT. *Nathaniel Hawthorne: The American Years*. New York, 1948.
   A second volume is projected.
CREWS, FREDERICK C. *The Sins of the Fathers: Hawthorne's Psychological Themes*. New York, 1966.
FOGLE, RICHARD HARTER. *Hawthorne's Fiction*. Norman, Oklahoma, 1952.
KAUL, A. N., ed. *Hawthorne: A Collection of Critical Essays*. Englewood Cliffs, New Jersey, 1966.
   Essays by various critics.
MALE, ROY R. *Hawthorne's Tragic Vision*. Austin, Texas, 1957.
MARTIN, TERENCE J. *Nathaniel Hawthorne*. New York, 1965.
STEWART, RANDALL. *Nathaniel Hawthorne: A Biography*. New Haven, 1948.
   Standard.
TURNER, ARLIN. *Nathaniel Hawthorne: An Introduction and Interpretation*. New York, 1961.
WAGGONER, HYATT H. *Hawthorne: A Critical Study*. Revised ed. Cambridge, Massachusetts, 1963.

HENRY WADSWORTH LONGFELLOW (1807–1882)

Editions

CANBY, HENRY SEIDEL. *Favorite Poems*. Garden City, New York, 1967.
LONGFELLOW, SAMUEL. *Works*. 14 vols. Boston, 1886–1891.
   Standard.

Biography and Criticism

ARVIN, NEWTON. *Longfellow*. Boston, 1963.
   Definitive.
LONGFELLOW, SAMUEL. *The Life of Henry W. Longfellow*. 2 vols. Boston, 1886.
   An additional volume was issued in 1887.

THOMPSON, LAWRANCE. *Young Longfellow, 1807–1843.* New York, 1938.

WAGENKNECHT, EDWARD. *Longfellow.* New York, 1955.

JOHN GREENLEAF WHITTIER (1807–1892)

Editions

CLARK, HARRY H. *Representative Selections.* New York, 1935. Convenient.

SCUDDER, HORACE E. *Writings.* 7 vols. Boston, 1894. Standard.

Biography and Criticism

LEARY, LEWIS. *John Greenleaf Whittier.* New York, 1962.

MORDELL, ALBERT. *Quaker Militant.* Boston, 1933.

PICKARD, SAMUEL T. *Life and Letters.* 2 vols. Revised ed. Boston, 1907.

POLLARD, JOHN A. *John Greenleaf Whittier.* Boston, 1949.

OLIVER WENDELL HOLMES (1809–1894)

Editions

———. *Works.* 13 vols. Boston, 1892.
Two additional volumes, John T. Morse's *Life and Letters,* were issued in 1896.

HAYAKAWA, SAMUEL, and HOWARD MUMFORD JONES. *Representative Selections.* New York, 1939. Convenient.

SCUDDER, HORACE E. *Complete Poetical Works.* Boston, 1895.

Biography and Criticism

HOWE, MARK A. DE WOLFE. *Holmes of the Breakfast Table.* New York, 1939.

SMALL, MIRIAM. *Oliver Wendell Holmes.* New York, 1962.

TILTON, ELEANOR M. *Amiable Autocrat.* New York, 1947.

ABRAHAM LINCOLN (1809–1865)

Editions

ANGLE, PAUL N., and EARL SCHENCK MIERS. *The Living Lincoln.* New Brunswick, New Jersey, 1955.
Distilled from the definitive Basler edition.

BASLER, ROY P., et al. *Collected Works.* 8 vols. New Brunswick, New Jersey, 1953. *Index,* 1955.
Definitive.
BASLER, ROY P. *Speeches and Writings.* Cleveland, 1946.
A convenient selection.

Biography and Criticism

CHARNWOOD, Lord. *Abraham Lincoln.* London, 1916.
HERNDON, WILLIAM H. *Life of Lincoln.* Revised ed. Greenwich, Connecticut, 1961.
A reedited version of the 1889 classic.
RANDALL, J. G. *Lincoln the President.* 2 vols. New York, 1945.
Continued by *Lincoln and the South* (1946) and *Lincoln, the Liberal Statesman* (1947).
SANDBURG, CARL. *Abraham Lincoln.* 6 vols. New York, 1926, 1939.
A classic, subsequently abridged in one volume.
THOMAS, BENJAMIN P. *Abraham Lincoln.* New York, 1952.
Highly regarded.

EDGAR ALLAN POE (1809–1849)

Editions

ALLERTON, MARGARET, and HARDIN CRAIG. *Representative Selections.* New York, 1935.
HARRISON, JAMES A. *Complete Works.* 17 vols. New York, 1902.
Reprinted in 1965.
OSTROM, JOHN W. *Letters.* 2 vols. Cambridge, Massachusetts, 1948.
QUINN, ARTHUR HOBSON, and EDWARD H. O'NEILL. *Complete Poems and Stories.* 2 vols. New York, 1946.

Biography and Criticism

DAVIDSON, EDWARD H. *Poe: A Critical Study.* Cambridge, Massachusetts, 1957.
PARKS, EDD WINFIELD. *Edgar Allan Poe as Literary Critic.* Atlanta, Georgia, 1964.
QUINN, ARTHUR HOBSON. *Edgar Allan Poe: A Critical Biography.* New York, 1941.
Standard.
REGAN, ROBERT, ed. *Poe: A Collection of Critical Essays.* Englewood Cliffs, New Jersey, 1967.
Essays by various critics.

WAGENKNECHT, EDWARD. *Edgar Allan Poe: The Man Behind the Legend.* New York, 1963.

HENRY DAVID THOREAU (1817–1862)

Editions

BLAKE, HARRISON G. O. *Complete Works.* 5 vols. Boston, 1929.
BODE, CARL. *Collected Poems.* Revised ed. Baltimore, 1964.
BODE, CARL, and WALTER HARDING. *Correspondence.* New York, 1958.
———. *The Portable Thoreau.* New York, 1947.
Convenient.
CANBY, HENRY SEIDEL. *Works.* Boston, 1937.
Convenient.
SANBORN, FRANK B., et al. *Writings.* 20 vols. Boston, 1906.
Standard. A new edition of the *Journals* section of the works was issued in 1949, edited by Francis H. Allen.

Biography and Criticism

CANBY, HENRY SEIDEL. *Thoreau.* Boston, 1939.
COOK, REGINALD L. *Passage to Walden.* Boston, 1949.
HARDING, WALTER. *The Days of Henry Thoreau.* New York, 1965.
Standard.
———. *A Thoreau Handbook.* New York, 1959.
KRUTCH, JOSEPH WOOD. *Henry David Thoreau.* New York, 1948.
PAUL, SHERMAN. *The Shores of America.* Urbana, Illinois, 1958.
———, ed. *Thoreau: A Collection of Critical Essays.* Englewood Cliffs, New Jersey, 1962.
Essays by various critics.

JAMES RUSSELL LOWELL (1819–1891)

Editions

CLARK, HARRY H., and NORMAN FOERSTER. *Representative Selections.* New York, 1947.
Convenient.
NORTON, CHARLES ELIOT. *Complete Writings.* 16 vols. Boston, 1904.
SMITH, THELMA M. *Uncollected Poems.* Philadelphia, 1950.

Biography and Criticism

BEATTY, RICHMOND C. *James Russell Lowell.* Nashville, Tennessee, 1942.

DUBERMAN, MARTIN B. *James Russell Lowell.* Boston, 1966.

HOWARD, LEON. *Victorian Knight-Errant.* Berkeley, 1952.

SCUDDER, HORACE E. *James Russell Lowell.* 2 vols. Cambridge, Massachusetts, 1901.

HERMAN MELVILLE (1819–1891)

Editions

CHASE, RICHARD. *Selected Tales and Poems.* New York, 1952.

HAYFORD, HARRISON, et al. *Writings.* Evanston, Illinois, 1968– .
The Northwestern-Newberry edition, in progress. *Typee, Omoo,* and *Redburn* have been issued to date.

HAYFORD, HARRISON, and HERSCHEL PARKER. *Moby-Dick.* New York, 1967.
The most reliable text produced to date.

OLIVER, EGBERT S., et al. *Complete Works,* Chicago, 1948– .
Of fourteen projected volumes, five have been issued, but the enterprise seems to have been abandoned. The Northwestern-Newberry edition promises to be definitive.

WEAVER, RAYMOND M. *Works.* 16 vols. London, 1922–1924.

Biography and Criticism

ARVIN, NEWTON. *Herman Melville.* New York, 1950.
Excellent.

BERTHOFF, WARNER. *The Example of Melville.* Princeton, 1962.

CHASE, RICHARD. *Herman Melville.* New York, 1949.

———, ed. *Melville: A Collection of Critical Essays.* Englewood Cliffs, New Jersey, 1962.
Essays by various critics.

HILLWAY, TYRUS, and LUTHER S. MANVILLE, eds. *Moby-Dick: Centennial Essays.* Dallas, 1953.

HOWARD, LEON. *Herman Melville.* Berkeley, 1951.

LEYDA, JAY. *The Melville Log.* 2 vols. New York, 1951.

MILLER, JAMES E., JR. *A Reader's Guide to Herman Melville.* New York, 1962.

OLSON, CHARLES. *Call Me Ishmael.* New York, 1947.

SEDGWICK, WILLIAM ELLERY. *Herman Melville.* Cambridge, 1944.

STERN, MILTON R. *The Fine Hammered Steel of Herman Melville.*
Urbana, Illinois, 1957.

VINCENT, HOWARD P. *The Trying-Out of Moby Dick.* Boston,
1949.

WALT WHITMAN (1819–1892)

Editions

ALLEN, GAY WILSON, et al. *Collected Writings.* New York,
1961–   .
The definitive edition, to be completed in fifteen volumes, of
which seven have appeared to date.

ALLEN, GAY WILSON, and CHARLES T. DAVIS. *Poems.* New York,
1955.
Well annotated.

BOWERS, FREDSON. *Whitman's Manuscripts: "Leaves of Grass"*
(*1860*). Chicago, 1955.

MILLER, JAMES E., JR. *Complete Poetry and Selected Prose.*
Boston, 1959.

Biography and Criticism

ALLEN, GAY WILSON. *The Solitary Singer.* New York, 1955.

———. *Walt Whitman Handbook.* Revised ed. New York, 1957.

ASSELINEAU, ROGER. *The Evolution of Walt Whitman.* 2 vols. Cambridge, Massachusetts, 1960, 1962.

CHASE, RICHARD. *Walt Whitman Reconsidered.* New York, 1955.

MILLER, EDWARD. *Walt Whitman's Poetry: A Psychological Journey.* Boston, 1968.

MILLER, JAMES E., JR. *Walt Whitman.* New York, 1962.

PEARCE, ROY HARVEY, ed. *Whitman: A Collection of Critical Essays.* Englewood Cliffs, New Jersey, 1962.
Essays by various critics.

HENRY TIMROD (1828–1867)

Editions

PARKS, EDD WINFIELD. *Essays.* Athens, Georgia, 1942.

PARKS, EDD WINFIELD, and AILEEN WELLS PARKS. *Collected Poems.*
Athens, Georgia, 1965.

Biography and Criticism

PARKS, EDD WINFIELD. *Henry Timrod.* New York, 1964.

EMILY DICKINSON (1830–1886)

Editions

JOHNSON, THOMAS H., and THEODORA WARD. *Letters*. 3 vols. Cambridge, Massachusetts, 1958.
JOHNSON, THOMAS H. *Complete Poems*. Boston, 1960.

Biography

JOHNSON, THOMAS H. *Emily Dickinson*. Cambridge, Massachusetts, 1955.

Criticism

ANDERSON, CHARLES R. *Emily Dickinson's Poetry*. New York, 1960.
CHASE, RICHARD. *Emily Dickinson*. New York, 1951.
GELPI, ALBERT. *Emily Dickinson*. Cambridge, Massachusetts, 1965.
GRIFFITH, CLARK. *The Long Shadow: Emily Dickinson's Tragic Poetry*. Princeton, 1964.
MILLER, RUTH. *The Poetry of Emily Dickinson*. Middletown, Connecticut, 1968.
SEWALL, RICHARD, ed. *Emily Dickinson: A Collection of Critical Essays*. Englewood Cliffs, New Jersey, 1963.
  Essays by various critics.
SHERWOOD, WILLIAM R. *Circumference and Circumstance*. New York, 1968.
WHICHER, GEORGE F. *This Was a Poet*. New York, 1938.

SAMUEL LANGHORNE CLEMENS (MARK TWAIN, 1835–1910)

Editions

DE VOTO, BERNARD. *The Portable Mark Twain*. New York, 1946.
NEIDER, CHARLES. *Autobiography*. Revised ed. New York, 1959.
———. *Complete Essays*. Garden City, New York, 1963.
———. *Complete Novels*. 2 vols. Garden City, New York, 1964.
———. *Complete Short Stories*. New York, 1957.
PAINE, ALBERT B. *Mark Twain's Letters*. 2 vols. New York, 1917.
  Additional letters are contained in Bernard De Voto's *Mark Twain in Eruption* (New York, 1940) as well as in Paine's biography, listed below.
———. *Writings*. 37 vols. New York, 1922–1925.

Biography and Criticism

BELLAMY, GLADYS CARMEN. *Mark Twain as a Literary Artist.* Norman, Oklahoma, 1950.

BLAIR, WALTER. *Mark Twain and Huck Finn.* Berkeley, 1960. Well regarded.

BROOKS, VAN WYCK. *The Ordeal of Mark Twain.* Revised ed. New York, 1933.

COX, JAMES M. *Mark Twain: The Fate of Humor.* Princeton, 1966.

DE VOTO, BERNARD. *Mark Twain's America.* Boston, 1932.

————. *Mark Twain at Work.* Cambridge, Massachusetts, 1942.

FERGUSON, J. DE LANCEY. *Mark Twain.* Indianapolis, Indiana, 1943.

KAPLAN, JUSTIN, ed. *Mark Twain: A Profile.* New York, 1967. Essays by various critics.

LONG, E. HUDSON. *Mark Twain Handbook.* New York, 1957.

PAINE, ALBERT B. *Mark Twain.* 3 vols. New York, 1912.

SCOTT, ARTHUR L., ed. *Mark Twain: Selected Criticism.* Dallas, 1955. Essays by various critics.

SMITH, HENRY NASH, ed. *Mark Twain: A Collection of Critical Essays.* Englewood Cliffs, New Jersey, 1963. Essays by various critics.

————. *Mark Twain: The Development of a Writer.* Cambridge, Massachusetts, 1962. Excellent.

WAGENKNECHT, EDWARD C. *Mark Twain.* New Haven, 1935.

WECTER, DIXON. *Sam Clemens of Hannibal.* Boston, 1952.

BRET HARTE (1836–1902)

Editions

————. *Writings.* 19 vols. Boston, 1896–1914. Of several collected editions this is probably the best.

HARRISON, JOSEPH B. *Representative Selections.* New York, 1941.

Biography and Criticism

DUCKETT, MARGARET. *Mark Twain and Bret Harte.* Norman, Oklahoma, 1964.

STEWART, GEORGE R., JR. *Bret Harte.* Boston, 1931.

WILLIAM DEAN HOWELLS (1837–1920)

Editions

COMMAGER, HENRY STEELE. *Selected Writings.* New York, 1950.
HOWELLS, MILDRED. *Life in Letters.* 2 vols. New York, 1928.
KIRK, CLARA MARBURG, and RUDOLPH KIRK. *Criticism and Fiction and Other Essays.* New York, 1959.
————. *Representative Selections.* New York, 1950.

Biography and Criticism

BROOKS, VAN WYCK. *Howells.* New York, 1959.
CADY, EDWIN H. *The Road to Realism.* Syracuse, New York, 1956. Continued, and concluded, by the same author's *The Realist at War* (1958). This is the definitive biography.
CARTER, EVERETT. *Howells and the Age of Realism.* Philadelphia, 1954.
KIRK, CLARA. *W. D. Howells.* New Brunswick, New Jersey, 1965.
VANDERBILT, KERMIT. *The Achievement of William Dean Howells: A Reinterpretation.* Princeton, 1968.

HENRY ADAMS (1838–1918)

Editions

ADAMS, JAMES TRUSLOW. *The Education of Henry Adams.* New York, 1946.
ARVIN, NEWTON. *Selected Letters.* New York, 1951.
STEVENSON, ELIZABETH. *A Henry Adams Reader.* New York, 1958.

Biography and Criticism

HOCHFIELD, GEORGE. *Henry Adams: An Introduction and an Interpretation.* New York, 1962.
LEVINSON, J. C. *The Mind and Art of Henry Adams.* Boston, 1957.
SAMUELS, ERNEST. *Henry Adams.* 3 vols. Cambridge, Massachusetts, 1948–1964.
    Standard.
STEVENSON, ELIZABETH. *Henry Adams: A Biography.* New York, 1955.

WILLIAM JAMES (1842–1910)

Edition

McDermot, John J. *Writings*. New York, 1967.

Biography and Criticism

Moore, Edward C. *William James*. New York, 1965.
Perry, Ralph Barton. *The Thought and Character of William James*. 2 vols. Boston, 1935.
   Later abridged and issued in one volume.

SIDNEY LANIER (1842–1881)

Editions

Anderson, Charles R., et al. *Centennial Edition*. 10 vols. Boston, 1945.
Young, Stark. *Selected Poems*. New York, 1947.

Biography and Criticism

Mims, Edwin. *Sidney Lanier*. Boston, 1905.
Starke, Aubrey H. *Sidney Lanier*. Chapel Hill, North Carolina, 1933.

HENRY JAMES (1843–1916)

Editions

————. *The Novels and Tales*. 26 vols. New York, 1907–1917. This is the famous "New York Edition," with texts revised by the author and prefaces. The London reprint of this edition (35 vols., 1921–1923) contains a number of added titles.
Blackmur, R. P. *The Art of the Novel*. New York, 1934.
   A collection of the prefaces to the New York edition.
Edel, Leon. *Complete Tales*. 12 vols. Philadelphia, 1962–1965.
————. *Selected Letters*. Garden City, New York, 1960.
Matthiessen, F. O. *The American Novels and Tales*. New York, 1947.
Matthiessen, F. O., and Kenneth Murdock. *Notebooks*. New York, 1947.
Richardson, Lyon. *Representative Selections*. New York, 1941.

Biography

EDEL, LEON. *Henry James.* Philadelphia, 1953– .
  The definitive biography. Four volumes, covering the years
  1843–1901, have been issued to date.

Criticism

CREWS, FREDERICK C. *The Tragedy of Manners.* New Haven, 1957.
DUPEE, F. W. *Henry James.* Revised ed. New York, 1956.
  An excellent brief introduction, biographically organized.
EDEL, LEON, ed. *Henry James: A Collection of Critical Essays.*
  Englewood Cliffs, New Jersey, 1963.
  Essays by various critics.
GARD, ROGER, ed. *Henry James: The Critical Heritage.* London,
  1968.
  Essays by various critics.
HOLLAND, LAURENCE. *The Expense of Vision: Essays on the Craft
  of Henry James.* Princeton, 1964.
KROOK, DOROTHEA. *The Ordeal of Consciousness in Henry James.*
  Cambridge, 1962.
MATTHIESSEN, F. O. *Henry James: The Major Phase.* New York,
  1944.
———. *The James Family.* New York, 1947.
POIRIER, RICHARD. *The Comic Sense of Henry James.* New York,
  1960.
PUTT, S. GORLEY. *Henry James: A Reader's Guide.* Ithaca, New
  York, 1968.
  Extremely useful.
STONE, EDWARD. *The Battle and the Books.* Athens, Ohio, 1964.
TANNER, TONY, ed. *Henry James: Modern Judgments.* London,
  1968.
  Essays by various critics.

GEORGE WASHINGTON CABLE (1844–1925)

Editions

———. *The Grandissimes.* New York, 1893.
BIKLÉ, LUCY L. C. *Old Creole Days.* New York, 1937.
TURNER, ARLIN. *The Negro Question.* New York, 1958.

Biography and Criticism

BIKLÉ, LUCY L. C. *George W. Cable: His Life and Letters.* New York, 1928.
By his daughter.
TURNER, ARLIN. *George W. Cable.* Durham, North Carolina, 1956.

JOEL CHANDLER HARRIS (1848–1908)

Editions

HARRIS, JULIA C. *Miscellaneous Literary, Political, and Social Writings.* Chapel Hill, North Carolina, 1931.
VAN SANTVOORD, GEORGE, and ARCHIBALD C. COOLIDGE. *The Favorite Uncle Remus.* Boston, 1948.

Biography and Criticism

BROOKES, STELLA BREWER. *Joel Chandler Harris.* Athens, Georgia, 1950.
COUSINS, PAUL M. *Joel Chandler Harris: A Biography.* Baton Rouge, Louisiana, 1968.
HARLOW, ALVIN F. *Joel Chandler Harris.* New York, 1941.
HARRIS, JULIA C. *Life and Letters.* Boston, 1918.
Standard.

SARAH ORNE JEWETT (1849–1909)

Editions

———. *Stories and Tales.* 7 vols. Boston, 1910.
CATHER, WILLA. *The Best Stories.* 2 vols. Boston, 1925.

Biography and Criticism

CARY, RICHARD. *Sarah Orne Jewett.* New York, 1962.
MATTHIESSEN, F. O. *Sarah Orne Jewett.* Boston, 1929.

WILLIAM VAUGHN MOODY (1869–1910)

Editions

LOVETT, ROBERT MORSS. *Selected Poems.* Boston, 1931.
MANLY, JOHN M. *Poems and Plays.* 2 vols. Boston, 1912.

Biography and Criticism

HALPERN, MARTIN. *William Vaughn Moody.* New York, 1964.
HENRY, DAVID D. *William Vaughn Moody.* Boston, 1934.

FRANK NORRIS (1870–1902)

Editions

————. *Complete Works.* 10 vols. Garden City, New York, 1928.
COLLINS, CARREL. *McTeague: A Story of San Francisco.* New York, 1950.
LYNN, KENNETH. *The Octopus: A Story of California.* Boston, 1958.
PIZER, DONALD. *Literary Criticism.* Austin, Texas, 1964.
WALKER, FRANKLIN. *Letters.* San Francisco, 1956.

Biography and Criticism

MARCHAND, ERNEST. *Frank Norris.* Stanford, California, 1942.
WALKER, FRANKLIN. *Frank Norris: A Biography.* New York, 1932.

The Twentieth Century

POLITICAL AND SOCIAL HISTORY

LINK, ARTHUR S., et al. *American Epoch: A History of the United States Since the 1890's*. 3rd ed. New York, 1967.
See also the works listed under the general heading, p. 111.

EDITH WHARTON (1862–1937)

Editions

ANDREWS, WAYNE. *The Best Short Stories*. New York, 1958.
QUINN, ARTHUR HOBSON. *An Edith Wharton Treasury*. New York, 1950.

Biography and Criticism

GRIFFITH, GRACE. *The Two Lives of Edith Wharton*. New York, 1965.
HOWE, IRVING, ed. *Edith Wharton: A Collection of Critical Essays*. Englewood Cliffs, New Jersey, 1962.
Essays by various critics.
LUBBOCK, PERCY. *Portrait of Edith Wharton*. New York, 1947.
NEVIUS, BLAKE. *Edith Wharton*. Berkeley, 1953.

HAMLIN GARLAND (1869–1940)

Editions

McCOMB, E. H. K. *A Son of the Middle Border*. New York, 1927.
McELDERRY, B. R. *Main-Travelled Roads*. New York, 1956.

Biography and Criticism

HOLLOWAY, JEAN. *Hamlin Garland*. Austin, Texas, 1960.

EDGAR LEE MASTERS (1869–1950)

Editions

———. *Across Spoon River: An Autobiography*. New York, 1936.
———. *Spoon River Anthology*. New ed. New York, 1961.

Biography and Criticism

HARTLEY, LOIS TEAL. *Spoon River Revisited.* Muncie, Indiana, 1963.

EDWIN ARLINGTON ROBINSON (1869–1935)

Editions

————. *Collected Poems.* New York, 1937.
TORRENCE, RIDGELY. *Selected Letters.* New York, 1940.
ZABEL, MORTON DAUWEN. *Selected Poems.* New York, 1965.

Biography and Criticism

ANDERSON, WALLACE L. *Edwin Arlington Robinson.* Boston, 1967.
COXE, LOUIS. *Edwin Arlington Robinson: The Life of Poetry.* New York, 1969.
FUSSELL, EDWIN S. *Edwin Arlington Robinson.* Berkeley, 1954.
NEFF, EMORY. *Edwin Arlington Robinson.* New York, 1948.
SMITH, CHARD P. *Where the Light Falls.* New York, 1965.
WINTERS, YVOR. *Edwin Arlington Robinson.* Norfolk, Connecticut, 1946.

STEPHEN CRANE (1871–1900)

Editions

FOLLETT, WILSON. *Collected Poems.* New York, 1930.
————. *Work[s].* 12 vols. New York, 1925–1926.
KATZ, JOSEPH. *The Portable Stephen Crane.* New York, 1969.
Contains *The Red Badge of Courage, Maggie, George's Mother,* short stories, poems, letters.

Biography and Criticism

BASSAN, MAURICE, ed. *Stephen Crane: A Collection of Critical Essays.* Englewood Cliffs, New Jersey, 1967.
Essays by various critics.
BERRYMAN, JOHN. *Stephen Crane.* New York, 1950.
HOFFMAN, DANIEL G. *The Poetry of Stephen Crane.* New York, 1957.
SOLOMON, ERIC. *Stephen Crane, from Parody to Realism.* Cambridge, Massachusetts, 1966.
STALLMAN, R. W. *Stephen Crane: A Biography.* New York, 1968.

THEODORE DREISER (1871-1945)

Editions

————. *An American Tragedy.* 2 vols. New York, 1925.
————. *The Bulwark.* Garden City, New York, 1946.
————. *The Financier.* New York, 1912.
————. *The "Genius."* New York, 1915.
————. *Jennie Gerhardt.* New York, 1911.
————. *The Stoic.* Garden City, New York, 1947.
————. *The Titan.* New York, 1914.
ELIAS, ROBERT H. *Letters.* 3 vols. Philadelphia, 1959.
FARRELL, JAMES T. *Best Short Stories.* Cleveland, 1956.
SIMPSON, CLAUDE. *Sister Carrie.* Boston, 1959.

Biography and Criticism

ELIAS, ROBERT H. *Theodore Dreiser.* New York, 1949.
KAZIN, ALFRED, and CHARLES SHAPIRO, eds. *The Stature of Theodore Dreiser.* Bloomington, Indiana, 1955.
  Essays by various critics.
MCALEER, JOHN J. *Theodore Dreiser: An Introduction and Interpretation.* New York, 1968.
MATTHIESSEN, F. O. *Theodore Dreiser.* New York, 1951.
SWANBERG, W. A. *Dreiser.* New York, 1965.

WILLA CATHER (1873-1947)

Editions

————. *April Twilight and Other Poems.* New York, 1933.
————. *Novels and Stories.* 13 vols. Boston, 1937-1941.

Biography and Criticism

BLOOM, EDWARD A., and LILLIAN D. BLOOM. *Willa Cather's Gift of Sympathy.* Carbondale, Illinois, 1962.
BROWN, E. K., and LEON EDEL. *Willa Cather.* New York, 1953.
RANDALL, JOHN HERMAN. *The Landscape and the Looking Glass.* Boston, 1960.
SERGEANT, ELIZABETH SHEPLEY. *Willa Cather.* Lincoln, Nebraska, 1963.

ROBERT FROST (1874–1963)

Editions

————. *Complete Poems.* New York, 1949.

————. *In the Clearing.* New York, 1962.

COX, HYDE, and EDWARD CONNERY LATHAM. *Selected Prose.* New York, 1966.

GRAVES, ROBERT. *Selected Poems.* New York, 1963.

THOMPSON, LAWRANCE R. *Selected Letters.* New York, 1964.

Biography and Criticism

BROWER, REUBEN. *The Poetry of Robert Frost.* New York, 1963. Excellent.

COOK, REGINALD L. *The Dimensions of Robert Frost.* New York, 1958.

COX, JAMES M., ed. *Robert Frost: A Collection of Critical Essays.* Englewood Cliffs, New Jersey, 1962.
Essays by various critics.

COX, SIDNEY. *A Swinger of Birches: A Portrait of Robert Frost.* New York, 1957.

SERGEANT, ELIZABETH SHEPLEY. *Robert Frost.* New York, 1960.

SQUIRES, RADCLIFFE. *The Major Themes of Robert Frost.* Ann Arbor, 1963.

THOMPSON, LAWRANCE. *Robert Frost.* New York, 1966– .
The definitive biography, of which the first volume, covering the years 1874–1915, has appeared.

ELLEN GLASGOW (1874–1945)

Editions

————. *Works.* 12 vols. New York, 1938.

MEEKER, RICHARD K. *The Collected Stories.* Baton Rouge, Louisiana, 1963.

ROUSE, BLAIR. *Letters.* New York, 1958.

Biography and Criticism

AUCHINCLOSS, LOUIS. *Ellen Glasgow.* Minneapolis, 1964.

MCDOWELL, FREDERICK P. W. *Ellen Glasgow.* Madison, Wisconsin, 1960.

SANTAS, JOAN FOSTER. *Ellen Glasgow's American Dream.* Charlottesville, Virginia, 1965.

JACK LONDON (1876–1916)

Editions

————. *Best Short Stories*. Garden City, New York, 1953.

FONER, PHILIP S. *Jack London, American Rebel: A Collection of His Social Writings*. New York, 1967.
Includes "an extensive study of the man and his times."

HENDRICKS, KING, and IRVING SHEPARD. *Letters*. New York, 1965.

SHEPARD, IRVING. *Tales of Adventure*. Garden City, New York, 1956.

Biography and Criticism

CALDER-MARSHALL, ARTHUR. *Lone Wolf*. New York, 1961.

FRANCHERE, RUTH. *Jack London: The Pursuit of a Dream*. New York, 1962.

O'CONNOR, RICHARD. *Jack London*. Boston, 1964.

SHERWOOD ANDERSON (1876–1941)

Editions

GREGORY, HORACE. *The Portable Sherwood Anderson*. New York, 1949.

JONES, HOWARD MUMFORD, and WALTER B. RIDEOUT. *Letters*. Boston, 1953.

ROSENFELD, PAUL. *The Sherwood Anderson Reader*. Boston, 1947.

WHITE, RAY LEWIS. *Memoirs*. Chapel Hill, North Carolina, 1969.

————. *A Story Teller's Story*. Cleveland, 1968.

Biography and Criticism

ANDERSON, DAVID D. *Sherwood Anderson*. New York, 1967.

BURBANK, REX. *Sherwood Anderson*. New York, 1964.

HOWE, IRVING. *Sherwood Anderson*. New York, 1951.

WHITE, RAY LEWIS, ed. *The Achievement of Sherwood Anderson*. Chapel Hill, North Carolina, 1966.
Essays by various critics.

CARL SANDBURG (1878–1967)

Editions

————. *Complete Poems*. New York, 1950.

————. *The Sandburg Range*. New York, 1957.

MITGANG, HERBERT. *Letters*. New York, 1968.

Biography and Criticism

CROWDER, RICHARD. *Carl Sandburg.* New York, 1964.

WALLACE STEVENS (1879–1955)

Editions

————. *Collected Poems.* New York, 1954.
MORSE, SAMUEL FRENCH. *Opus Posthumous.* New York, 1957.
STEVENS, HOLLY. *Letters.* New York, 1966.

Biography and Criticism

BAIRD, JAMES. *The Dome and the Rock: Structure in the Poetry of Wallace Stevens.* Baltimore, 1968.
BOROFF, MARIE, ed. *Wallace Stevens: A Collection of Critical Essays.* Englewood Cliffs, New Jersey, 1963.
  Essays by various critics.
BURNEY, WILLIAM A. *Wallace Stevens.* New York, 1968.
KERMODE, FRANK. *Wallace Stevens.* New York, 1961.
  Excellent.
PACK, ROBERT. *Wallace Stevens.* New Brunswick, New Jersey, 1958.
PEARCE, ROY HARVEY, and J. HILLIS MILLER, eds. *The Act of the Mind.* Baltimore, 1965.
  Essays by various critics.
RIDDEL, JOSEPH N. *The Clairvoyant Eye: The Poetry and Poetics of Wallace Stevens.* Baton Rouge, Louisiana, 1965.

VACHEL LINDSAY (1879–1931)

Editions

————. *Adventures, Rhymes, and Designs.* New York, 1968.
————. *Collected Poems.* Revised ed. New York, 1925.
————. *Selected Poems.* New York, 1963.

Biography and Criticism

MASTERS, EDGAR LEE. *Vachel Lindsay: A Poet in America.* New York, 1935.
RUGGLES, ELEANOR. *The West-Going Heart: A Life of Vachel Lindsay.* New York, 1959.

H. L. MENCKEN (1880–1956)

Editions

————. *Happy Days.* New York, 1940.
The first of three volumes of autobiography. The other two
are *Newspaper Days* (1941) and *Heathen Days* (1943).
————. *The Days.* New York, 1947.
CAIRNS, HUNTINGTON. *The American Scene.* New York, 1965.
FORGUE, GUY J. *Letters.* New York, 1961.
McHUGH, ROBERT. *The Bathtub Hoax and Other Blasts.* New York,
1958.
MOOS, MALCOLM. *A Carnival of Buncombe.* Baltimore, 1956.

Biography and Criticism

ANGOFF, CHARLES. *H. L. Mencken: A Portrait from Memory.* New
York, 1956.
MANCHESTER, WILLIAM. *Disturber of the Peace.* New York, 1951.
NOLTE, WILLIAM H. *H. L. Mencken, Literary Critic.* Middletown,
Connecticut, 1966.

WILLIAM CARLOS WILLIAMS (1883–1963)

Editions

————. *Collected Earlier Poems.* New York, 1951.
————. *Collected Later Poems.* Revised ed. New York, 1963.
————. *Selected Essays.* New York, 1954.
THIRLWALL, JOHN C. *Selected Letters.* New York, 1957.

Biography and Criticism

DIJKSTRA, BRAM. *The Hieroglyphics of a New Speech.* Princeton,
1969.
KOCH, VIVIENNE. *William Carlos Williams.* Norfolk, Connecticut,
1950.
MILLER, J. HILLIS, ed. *William Carlos Williams: A Collection of
Critical Essays.* Englewood Cliffs, New Jersey, 1966.
Essays by various critics.
OSTROM, ALAN B. *The Poetic World of William Carlos Williams.*
Carbondale, Illinois, 1966.
WAGNER, LINDA. *The Poems of William Carlos Williams.* Middle-
town, Connecticut, 1964.

SINCLAIR LEWIS (1885–1951)

Editions

————. *Novels*. New York, 1931.
> The four principal novels: *Main Street* (1920), *Babbitt* (1922), *Elmer Gantry* (1927), *Dodsworth* (1929).

MAULE, HARRY E., and MELVILLE H. CANE. *The Man from Main Street*. New York, 1953.
> The subtitle is *Selected Essays and Other Writings*.

SMITH, HARRISON. *From Main Street to Stockholm*. New York, 1952.
> Letters.

Biography and Criticism

DOOLEY, D. J. *The Art of Sinclair Lewis*. Lincoln, Nebraska, 1967.

SCHORER, MARK, ed. *Sinclair Lewis: A Collection of Critical Essays*. Englewood Cliffs, New Jersey, 1962.
> Essays by various critics.

————. *Sinclair Lewis: An American Life*. New York, 1961.
> Definitive.

EZRA POUND (1885–   )

Editions

————. *The Cantos*. New York, 1948.
> Subsequent Cantos were issued in 1954, 1956, and 1959.

————. *Personae: The Collected Poems*. New York, 1950.

ELIOT, T. S. *Literary Essays*. Norfolk, Connecticut, 1954.

————. *Selected Poems*. Revised ed. London, 1959.

PAIGE, D. D. *Letters*. New York, 1950.

Criticism

DAVIE, DONALD. *Ezra Pound: Poet as Sculptor*. New York, 1963.

DEKKER, GEORGE. *The Cantos of Ezra Pound*. New York, 1963.

KENNER, HUGH. *The Poetry of Ezra Pound*. Norfolk, Connecticut, 1951.

NORMAN, CHARLES. *The Case of Ezra Pound*. New York, 1968.

————. *Ezra Pound*. New York, 1960.

SUTTON, WALTER, ed. *Ezra Pound: A Collection of Critical Essays.*
Englewood Cliffs, New Jersey, 1963.
Essays by various critics.
WATTS, H. H. *Ezra Pound and the Cantos.* Chicago, 1952.

ROBINSON JEFFERS (1887–1962)

Editions

————. *Selected Poetry.* New York, 1938.
RIDGEWAY, ANN N. *Selected Letters.* Baltimore, 1968.

Biography and Criticism

CARPENTER, FREDERIC IVES. *Robinson Jeffers.* New York, 1962.
MONJIAN, M. C. *Robinson Jeffers.* Pittsburgh, 1958.
POWELL, LAWRENCE CLARK. *Robinson Jeffers.* Revised ed. Pasadena, California, 1940.
SQUIRES, RADCLIFFE. *The Loyalties of Robinson Jeffers.* Ann Arbor, 1956.

MARIANNE MOORE (1887–   )

Editions

————. *Complete Poems.* New York, 1967.
————. *A Marianne Moore Reader.* New York, 1961.

Criticism

ENGEL, BERNARD F. *Marianne Moore.* New York, 1964.
NITCHIE, GEORGE W. *Marianne Moore: An Introduction to the Poetry.* New York, 1969.
TOMLINSON, CHARLES, ed. *Marianne Moore: A Collection of Critical Essays.* Englewood Cliffs, New Jersey, 1969.
Essays by various critics.

T. S. ELIOT (1888–1965)

Editions

————. *Complete Poems and Plays.* London, 1969.
Contains all the published poems and the five plays.
————. *Selected Essays.* New York, 1950.

Biography and Criticism

FRYE, NORTHROP. *T. S. Eliot*. Edinburgh, 1963.
  An excellent brief introduction.
GARDNER, HELEN. *The Art of T. S. Eliot*. London, 1950.
  On the *Four Quartets*.
JONES, GENESIUS. *Approach to the Purpose*. London, 1964.
KENNER, HUGH, ed. *T. S. Eliot: A Collection of Critical Essays*.
    Englewood Cliffs, New Jersey, 1962.
  Essays by various critics.
MATTHIESSEN, F. O. *The Achievement of T. S. Eliot*. 3rd ed. New
    York, 1958.
SMITH, GROVER. *T. S. Eliot's Poetry and Plays*. Chicago, 1956.
SOUTHAM, B. C. *A Student's Guide to the Selected Poems*. London,
    1968.
TATE, ALLEN, ed. *T. S. Eliot: The Man and His Work*. New York,
    1953.
  A collection of essays by distinguished Eliot critics.
WILLIAMSON, GEORGE. *A Reader's Guide to T. S. Eliot*. New
    York, 1953.
  Useful though not always perfectly lucid.

JOHN CROWE RANSOM (1888–   )

Editions

————. *Poems and Essays*. New York, 1955.
————. *Selected Poems*. 2nd ed. New York, 1963.

Criticism

BUFFINGTON, ROBERT. *The Equilibrist*. Nashville, Tennessee,
    1967.
KNIGHT, KARL F. *The Poetry of John Crowe Ransom*. The Hague,
    1964.
YOUNG, THOMAS D., ed. *John Crowe Ransom: Critical Essays and
    a Bibliography*. Baton Rouge, Louisiana, 1968.

EUGENE O'NEILL (1888–1953)

Editions

————. *Plays*. 12 vols. New York, 1934–1935.
  O'Neill subsequently wrote *A Moon for the Misbegotten*
  (1947), *Long Day's Journey into Night* (1956), *A Touch of*

the Poet (1957), and *More Stately Mansions,* first produced in Stockholm in 1963.

————. *Selected Plays.* New York, 1969.

Ten plays.

GELLERT, LAWRENCE. *Lost Plays.* New York, 1950.

Biography and Criticism

CARGILL, OSCAR, et al., eds. *O'Neill and His Plays.* New York, 1961.

Essays by various critics.

ENGEL, EDWIN A. *The Haunted Heroes of Eugene O'Neill.* Cambridge, Massachusetts, 1953.

FALK, DORIS V. *Eugene O'Neill and the Tragic Tension.* New Brunswick, New Jersey, 1958.

GASSNER, JOHN, ed. *O'Neill: A Collection of Critical Essays.* Englewood Cliffs, New Jersey, 1964.

Essays by various critics.

GELB, ARTHUR, and BARBARA GELB. *O'Neill.* New York, 1962.

LEECH, CLIFFORD. *Eugene O'Neill.* New York, 1963.

RALEIGH, JOHN. *The Plays of Eugene O'Neill.* Carbondale, Illinois, 1965.

CONRAD AIKEN (1889–   )

Editions

————. *Collected Novels.* New York, 1964.

————. *Collected Poems.* New York, 1953.

Selected Poems was issued in 1961.

————. *Collected Short Stories.* London, 1966.

————. *A Reviewer's ABC: Collected Criticism.* London, 1961.

Biography and Criticism

HOFFMAN, FREDERICK J. *Conrad Aiken.* New York, 1962.

MARTIN, JAY. *Conrad Aiken: A Life of His Art.* Princeton, 1962.

HENRY MILLER (1891–   )

Edition

DURRELL, LAWRENCE. *The Henry Miller Reader.* New York, 1959.

Biography and Criticism

BAXTER, ANNETTE K. *Henry Miller, Expatriate.* Pittsburgh, 1961.
GORDON, WILLIAM A. *The Mind and Art of Henry Miller.* Baton Rouge, Louisiana, 1967.
WICKES, GEORGE, ed. *Henry Miller and the Critics.* Carbondale, Illinois, 1963.
   Essays by various critics.

ARCHIBALD MACLEISH (1892–   )

Editions

———. *Collected Poems.* Boston, 1952.
———. *A Continuing Journey.* Boston, 1968.
   Essays.

EDNA ST. VINCENT MILLAY (1892–1950)

Editions

MACDOUGALL, ALLEN ROSS. *Letters.* New York, 1952.
MILLAY, NORMA. *Collected Poems.* New York, 1956.

Biography and Criticism

BRITTIN, NORMAN A. *Edna St. Vincent Millay.* New York, 1967.
GURKO, MIRIAM. *Restless Spirit.* New York, 1962.
SHEEAN, VINCENT. *The Indigo Bunting.* New York, 1951.

E. E. CUMMINGS (1894–1962)

Editions

———. *Complete Poems.* 2 vols. London, 1968.
FIRMAGE, GEORGE JAMES. *E. E. Cummings: A Miscellany.* Revised ed. New York, 1965.
   Prose.

Biography and Criticism

FRIEDMAN, NORMAN. *E. E. Cummings.* Baltimore, 1960.
NORMAN, CHARLES. *The Magic-Maker.* Revised ed. New York, 1965.
WEGNER, ROBERT. *The Poetry and Prose of E. E. Cummings.* New York, 1965.

JAMES THURBER (1894–1961)

Editions

————. *The Thurber Album*. New York, 1952.
————. *The Thurber Carnival*. New York, 1945.

Biography

MORSBERGER, ROBERT E. *James Thurber*. New York, 1964.
TOBIAS, RICHARD C. *The Art of James Thurber*. Athens, Ohio, 1969.

JOHN DOS PASSOS (1896–   )

Edition

————. *U.S.A.* New York, 1937.
   The important trilogy, comprising *The 42nd Parallel, 1919,* and *The Big Money*.

Biography and Criticism

ASTRE, GEORGES-ALBERT. *Thèmes et structures dans l'oeuvre de John Dos Passos*. Paris, 1956.
WRENN, JOHN H. *John Dos Passos*. New York, 1962.

F. SCOTT FITZGERALD (1896–1940)

Editions

————. *The Bodley Head Scott Fitzgerald*. London, 1960–   .
   In progress.
COWLEY, MALCOLM. *The Stories*. New York, 1951.
MIZENER, ARTHUR. *The Fitzgerald Reader*. New York, 1963.
TURNBULL, ANDREW. *Letters*. New York, 1963.
   Supplemented by another volume, *Letters to His Daughter,* issued in 1965.
WILSON, EDMUND. *The Crack-Up*. Norfolk, Connecticut, 1945.
   Miscellaneous uncollected works.

Biography and Criticism

HINDUS, MILTON. *F. Scott Fitzgerald*. New York, 1968.
KAZIN, ALFRED, ed. *F. Scott Fitzgerald: The Man and His Work*. Cleveland, 1951.
   Essays by various critics.

LEHAN, RICHARD. *F. Scott Fitzgerald and the Craft of Fiction.* Carbondale, Illinois, 1966.

MILLER, JAMES E. *F. Scott Fitzgerald: His Art and Technique.* New York, 1964.

MIZENER, ARTHUR, ed. *F. Scott Fitzgerald: A Collection of Critical Essays.* Englewood Cliffs, New Jersey, 1963.
Essays by various critics.

MIZENER, ARTHUR. *The Far Side of Paradise.* 2nd ed. Boston, 1965.

PIPER, HENRY D. *F. Scott Fitzgerald.* New York, 1965.

TURNBULL, ANDREW. *Scott Fitzgerald.* New York, 1962.

WILLIAM FAULKNER (1897–1962)

Editions

————. *Collected Stories.* New York, 1950.

————. *The Faulkner Reader.* New York, 1954.

COWLEY, MALCOLM. *The Portable Faulkner.* New York, 1946.

MERIWETHER, JAMES B. *Essays, Speeches, and Public Letters.* New York, 1965.

Biography and Criticism

ADAMS, RICHARD P. *Faulkner: Myth and Motion.* Princeton, 1968.

BROOKS, CLEANTH. *William Faulkner.* New Haven, 1963.

HOFFMAN, FREDERICK J., and OLGA VICKERY. *William Faulkner: Two Decades of Criticism.* East Lansing, Michigan, 1960.
Essays by various critics.

HOWE, IRVING. *William Faulkner.* New York, 1952.

THOMPSON, LAWRANCE. *Faulkner: An Introduction.* 2nd ed. New York, 1967.

VICKERY, OLGA W. *The Novels of William Faulkner.* Baton Rouge, Louisiana, 1959.

VOLPE, EDMOND L. *A Reader's Guide to William Faulkner.* New York, 1964.

WAGGONER, HYATT H. *William Faulkner.* Lexington, Kentucky, 1959.

WARREN, ROBERT PENN, ed. *Faulkner: A Collection of Critical Essays.* Englewood Cliffs, New Jersey, 1966.
Essays by various critics.

THORNTON WILDER (1897–   )

Editions

————. *A Thornton Wilder Trio.* New York, 1956.
Contains *The Cabala, The Bridge of San Luis Rey, The Woman of Andros.*
————. *Three Plays.* New York, 1957.
Contains *Our Town, The Skin of Our Teeth, The Matchmaker.*

Biography and Criticism

BURBANK, REX. *Thornton Wilder.* New York, 1961.
GOLDSTEIN, MALCOLM. *The Art of Thornton Wilder.* Lincoln, Nebraska, 1965.
HABERMAN, DONALD. *The Plays of Thornton Wilder.* Middletown, Connecticut, 1967.

ERNEST HEMINGWAY (1898–1961)

Editions

————. *The Fifth Column and the First Forty-Nine Stories.* New York, 1938.
COWLEY, MALCOLM. *The Portable Hemingway.* New York, 1944.
POORE, CHARLES. *The Hemingway Reader.* New York, 1953.

Biography and Criticism

BAKER, CARLOS. *Ernest Hemingway: A Life Story.* New York, 1969.
————, ed. *Hemingway and His Critics.* New York, 1961.
Essays by various critics.
BAKER, SHERIDAN. *Ernest Hemingway.* New York, 1967.
ROSS, LILLIAN. *Portrait of Hemingway.* New York, 1961.
Malicious.
WEEKS, ROBERT P., ed. *Hemingway: A Collection of Critical Essays.* Englewood Cliffs, New Jersey, 1962.
Essays by various critics.
YOUNG, PHILIP. *Ernest Hemingway.* New York, 1952.
Highly regarded.

HART CRANE (1899–1932)

Editions

WEBER, BROM. *Complete Poems and Selected Letters.* London, 1969.

Biography and Criticism

BUTTERFIELD, R. W. *The Broken Arc: A Study of Hart Crane.* London, 1969.

LEIBOWITZ, HERBERT A. *Hart Crane: An Introduction to the Poetry.* New York, 1968.

LEWIS, R. W. B. *The Poetry of Hart Crane.* Princeton, 1967.

UNTERECKER, JOHN. *Voyager: A Life of Hart Crane.* New York, 1969.

WEBER, BROM. *Hart Crane.* New York, 1948.

ALLEN TATE (1899–   )

Editions

————. *Collected Essays.* Denver, 1959.

————. *The Fathers.* New York, 1938.

A novel, reissued in Denver, 1960.

————. *Poems.* New York, 1960.

Biography and Criticism

BISHOP, FERMAN. *Allen Tate.* New York, 1967.

MEINERS, R. K. *The Last Alternatives: A Study of the Works of Allen Tate.* Denver, 1963.

THOMAS WOLFE (1900–1938)

Editions

GEISMAR, MAXWELL. *The Portable Thomas Wolfe.* New York, 1946.

Subsequently issued as *The Indispensable Thomas Wolfe.*

HOLMAN, C. HUGH. *The Thomas Wolfe Reader.* New York, 1962.

NOWELL, ELIZABETH. *Letters.* New York, 1956.

Biography and Criticism

FIELD, LESLIE A., ed. *Thomas Wolfe: Three Decades of Criticism.* New York, 1968.

Essays by various critics.

JOHNSON, PAMELA HANSFORD. *Hungry Gulliver*. New York, 1948.
Subsequently issued as *The Art of Thomas Wolfe*.

KENNEDY, RICHARD S. *The Window of Memory*. Chapel Hill,
North Carolina, 1962.

MULLER, HERBERT J. *Thomas Wolfe*. Norfolk, Connecticut, 1947.

NOWELL, ELIZABETH. *Thomas Wolfe*. New York, 1960.

RUBIN, LOUIS D. *Thomas Wolfe*. Baton Rouge, Louisiana, 1955.

TURNBULL, ANDREW. *Thomas Wolfe*. New York, 1967.

WALSER, RICHARD, ed. *The Enigma of Thomas Wolfe*. Cambridge,
Massachusetts, 1953.
Essays by various critics.

WATKINS, FLOYD C. *Thomas Wolfe's Characters*. Norman, Oklahoma, 1957.

LANGSTON HUGHES (1902–1967)

Editions

————. *The Big Sea: An Autobiography*. New York, 1940.
Followed by *I Wonder as I Wander,* 1956.

————. *Five Plays*. Bloomington, Indiana, 1963.

————. *The Langston Hughes Reader*. New York, 1958.

————. *Selected Poems*. New York, 1959.

Biography and Criticism

DICKINSON, DONALD C. *A Bio-Bibliography of Langston Hughes*.
Hamden, Connecticut, 1967.

EMANUEL, JAMES A. *Langston Hughes*. New York, 1967.

JOHN STEINBECK (1902–1968)

Editions

COVICI, PASCAL. *The Portable Steinbeck*. New York, 1943.

JACKSON, JOSEPH HENRY. *Short Novels*. New York, 1953.

Biography and Criticism

LISCA, PETER. *The Wide World of John Steinbeck*. New Brunswick, New Jersey, 1958.

NATHANAEL WEST (1904–1940)

Edition

ROSS, ALAN. *Complete Works*. New York, 1957.

Biography and Criticism

COMERCHERO, VICTOR. *Nathanael West.* Syracuse, New York, 1964.

LIGHT, JAMES F. *Nathanael West.* Evanston, Illinois, 1961.

REID, RANDALL. *The Fiction of Nathanael West.* Chicago, 1967.

ROBERT PENN WARREN (1905–   )

Editions

————. *All the King's Men.* New York, 1946.
Reissued, with an introduction by the author, in 1953.

————. *Selected Essays.* New York, 1958.

————. *Selected Poems.* New York, 1966.

Biography and Criticism

BOHNER, CHARLES H. *Robert Penn Warren.* New York, 1964.

CASPER, LEONARD. *Robert Penn Warren.* Seattle, 1960.

LONGLEY, JOHN L., ed. *Robert Penn Warren: A Collection of Critical Essays.* New York, 1965.
Essays by various critics.

CLIFFORD ODETS (1906–1963)

Editions

————. *Six Plays.* New York, 1939.
Followed by *Night Music* (1940), *Clash by Night* (1942), *The Big Knife* (1949), and *The Country Girl* (1951).

Biography and Criticism

BENTLEY, ERIC. *The Playwright as Thinker.* New York, 1955.

MURRAY, EDWARD. *Clifford Odets: The Thirties and After.* New York, 1968.

SHUMAN, R. BAIRD. *Clifford Odets.* New York, 1962.

THEODORE ROETHKE (1908–1963)

Editions

————. *Collected Poems.* New York, 1966.

MILLS, RALPH J., JR. *On the Poet and His Craft.* Seattle, 1965.
Prose.

Biography and Criticism

MOLOFF, KARL. *Theodore Roethke*. New York, 1966.
SEAGER, ALLAN. *The Glass House: The Life of Theodore Roethke*.
New York, 1968.
STEIN, ARNOLD, ed. *Theodore Roethke*. Seattle, 1965.
Essays by various critics.

EUDORA WELTY (1909–   )

Edition

————. *Losing Battles*. New York, 1970.
————. *Selected Stories*. New York, 1954.

Biography and Criticism

VANDE KIEFT, RUTH. *Eudora Welty*. New York, 1962.

JOHN BERRYMAN (1914–   )

Editions

————. *Homage to Mistress Bradstreet*. London, 1959.
————. *77 Dream Songs*. New York, 1964.
————. *Short Poems*. New York, 1967.
————. *Sonnets*. New York, 1967.

BERNARD MALAMUD (1914–   )

Editions

————. *The Assistant*. New York, 1957.
————. *The Fixer*. New York, 1966.
————. *Idiots First*. New York, 1963.
————. *The Magic Barrel*. New York, 1958.
————. *A Malamud Reader*. New York, 1967.
————. *The Natural*. New York, 1952.
————. *A New Life*. New York, 1961.

Biography and Criticism

RICHMAN, SIDNEY. *Bernard Malamud*. New York, 1966.

SAUL BELLOW (1915–   )

Editions

————. *The Adventures of Augie March*. New York, 1953.
————. *Dangling Man*. New York, 1944.
————. *Henderson the Rain King*. New York, 1959.
————. *Herzog*. New York, 1964.
————. *Mosby's Memoirs*. New York, 1968.
  Short Stories.
————. *Mr. Sammler's Planet*. New York, 1970.
————. *The Victim*. New York, 1947.

Biography and Criticism

CLAYTON, JOHN J. *Saul Bellow*. Bloomington, Indiana, 1968.
MALIN, IRVING, ed. *Saul Bellow and the Critics*. New York, 1967.
  Essays by various critics.
————. *Saul Bellow's Fiction*. Carbondale, Illinois, 1969.
OPDAHL, KEITH. *The Novels of Saul Bellow*. University Park, Pennsylvania, 1967.

ARTHUR MILLER (1916–   )

Editions

————. *After the Fall*. New York, 1964.
————. *Collected Plays*. New York, 1957.
  Contains *All My Sons, Death of a Salesman, The Crucible, A Memory of Two Mondays,* and *A View from the Bridge*.
————. *I Don't Need You Any More: Stories*. New York, 1967.
————. *Incident at Vichy*. New York, 1965.
————. *The Misfits*. New York, 1961.

Biography and Criticism

CORRIGAN, ROBERT W., ed. *Arthur Miller: A Collection of Critical Essays*. Englewood Cliffs, New Jersey, 1969.
  Essays by various critics.
HUFTEL, SHEILA. *Arthur Miller: The Burning Glass*. New York, 1965.
MOSS, LEONARD. *Arthur Miller*. New York, 1967.

ROBERT LOWELL (1917–   )

Editions

——. *Near the Ocean.* New York, 1967.
——. *Selected Poems.* London, 1965.

Biography and Criticism

MAZZARO, JEROME. *The Poetic Themes of Robert Lowell.* Ann Arbor, 1965.
STAPLES, HUGH B. *Robert Lowell.* New York, 1962.

PETER TAYLOR (1917–   )

Editions

——. *The Collected Stories.* New York, 1969.
——. *Happy Families Are All Alike.* New York, 1960.
——. *Miss Leonora When Last Seen.* New York, 1963.
——. *The Widows of Thornton.* New York, 1954.
——. *A Woman of Means.* New York, 1950.

J. D. SALINGER (1919–   )

Editions

——. *The Catcher in the Rye.* Boston, 1951.
——. *Franny and Zooey.* Boston, 1961.
——. *Nine Stories.* New York, 1953.
——. *Raise High the Roof Beam, Carpenters.* Boston, 1963.

Biography and Criticism

FRENCH, WARREN. *J. D. Salinger.* New York, 1963.
GWYNN, FREDERICK L., and JOSEPH L. BLOTNER. *The Fiction of J. D. Salinger.* Pittsburgh, 1958.

RICHARD WILBUR (1921–   )

Edition

——. *Poems.* New York, 1963.

JAMES DICKEY (1923–   )

Editions

————. *Deliverance*. Boston, 1970.

————. *The Eye-Beaters, Blood, Victory, Madness, Buckhead, and Mercy*. Garden City, New York, 1970.

————. *Poems 1957–1967*. Middletown, Connecticut, 1967.

LIEBERMAN, LAURENCE. *The Achievement of James Dickey: A Comprehensive Selection*. Glenview, Illinois, 1968.

JAMES BALDWIN (1924–   )

Editions

————. *Another Country*. New York, 1962.

————. *Blues for Mister Charlie: A Play*. New York, 1964.

————. *The Fire Next Time*. New York, 1963.

————. *Giovanni's Room, a Novel*. New York, 1956.

————. *Going to Meet the Man*. New York, 1965.
Short Stories.

————. *Go Tell It on the Mountain*. New York, 1953.

————. *Nobody Knows My Name*. New York, 1961.

————. *Notes of a Native Son*. Boston, 1955.

————. *Tell Me How Long the Train's Been Gone*. New York, 1968.

Biography and Criticism

ECKMAN, FERN MARJA. *The Furious Passage of James Baldwin*. New York, 1966.
Mainly a biographical record, based on interviews.

FLANNERY O'CONNOR (1925–1964)

Editions

————. *Everything That Rises Must Converge*. New York, 1965.

————. *A Good Man Is Hard to Find*. New York, 1955.

————. *The Violent Bear It Away*. New York, 1960.

————. *Wise Blood*. 2nd ed. New York, 1962.

Biography and Criticism

DRAKE, ROBERT. *Flannery O'Connor.* Grand Rapids, Michigan, 1966.

FRIEDMAN, MELVIN J., and LEWIS A. LAWSON, eds. *The Added Dimension.* New York, 1966.
Essays by various critics.

General, Classical, and Modern European History and Literature

Reference Works

Cassell's Encyclopaedia of World Literature, ed. S. H. STEINBERG, 2 vols. New York, 1954.

Brief histories of literatures; articles on literary forms; biographies of world writers; altogether extremely useful.

Chambers's Biographical Dictionary, ed. J. O. THORNE. Revised ed. New York, 1961.

LANGER, WILLIAM L. *An Encyclopedia of World History.* 4th ed. Boston, 1968.

A splendid compilation, containing in economical compass most merely factual information (dates, reigns, wars) needful for literary study.

The Oxford Companion to American History, ed. THOMAS H. JOHNSON. New York, 1966.

The Oxford Companion to the Theatre, ed. PHYLLIS HARTNOLL. 3rd ed. Oxford, 1967.

Oriented to the theatrical rather than to the literary aspects of drama.

SHIPLEY, JOSEPH T. *Dictionary of World Literature.* Revised ed. New York, 1953.

A comprehensive and sometimes authoritative dictionary of definitions (and discussions) of critical terms of which R. S. Crane's article on "Neo-classic Criticism" is a classic.

————. *Encyclopedia of Literature.* 2 vols. New York, 1946.

A series of articles on national literatures ("African Literature," "Albanian Literature"), concluding with a number of skimpy biographies of literary figures.

Dictionaries

Greek

A Greek-English Lexicon, ed. HENRY GEORGE LIDDELL and ROBERT
   SCOTT. Revised ed. Oxford, 1940.
   Standard, but does not contain English-Greek section.

Latin

Cassell's New Latin-English, English-Latin Dictionary, ed. D. P.
   SIMPSON. London, 1959.

French

The New Cassell's French Dictionary, ed. DENIS GIRARD et al.
   New York, 1962.

German

Cassell's German and English Dictionary, ed. HAROLD T. BETT-
   RIDGE. London, 1957.

Spanish

Cassell's Spanish Dictionary, ed. ALISON PEERS et al. London, 1959.

Cultural and Intellectual History

BRINTON, CRANE. *Ideas and Men: The Story of Western Thought.* New York, 1950.

RANDALL, JOHN HERMAN, JR. *The Making of the Modern Mind.* Revised ed. New York, 1940.

Originally issued in 1926, this work is now inevitably somewhat dated.

Index of English and American Authors

29566

DATE DUE